Words
Aptly
Spoken

Words Aptly Spoken

by
Dr. Bob Moorehead

Overlake Christian Press
Kirkland, Washington

Unless otherwise noted, the Bible version used in this publication is The Holy Bible: New International Version. Copyright 1973,1978, 1984 International Bible Society. Used by permission of Zondervan Bible Publishers.

Overlake Christian Press

9051 132nd Avenue N.E., Kirkland, Washington 98033

Printed in the United States of America

ISBN   0-9639496-6-7

This book is dedicated to Mary Young, my friend, encourager, and secretary from 1972 until 1992 when she retired. She was the original typist on most of the monologues found in this volume. Her untiring patience, and willing sweet spirit made it possible for me to write these monologues initially.

CONTENTS

**HRISTIANITY**

The Christianity of the Book of Acts and the Christianity most people see today seem worlds apart! What was it that made that early Church out live, out love, out pray, out work and out give their Roman pagan contemporaries? I think I know...it was a sense of "do or die." Christianity didn't just "blend in with the woodwork" in the first century. It was bold, aggressive, deliberate, dynamic, and it penetrated into the culture of the day. We need a fresh baptism today of that brand of Christianity!

AUTHENTICITY

I want authentic Christianity! Submerge the substitutes! Cancel the counterfeits! Forever forfeit the fake, the phony! I yearn for the real, not the redundant; the revolutionary, not the respectable; the royal, not the residual; the radical, not the regular.

I have not been born again, saved from sin, raised to life and changed forever just to contemplate, cloister and co-chair committees; I am here to win, not match; march, not meander; soar, not slide; claim, not capitulate; climb, not crawl. I'm redeemed to run, not retreat; to rush, not rest; to race, not rust; to advance not acquiesce.

I want to be propelled by power, prepared by prayer, prompted by passion, pruned by purity and primed by presence. I long for the lingering, lilting, lasting love for my Lord. I passionately desire a hatred for the insipid, the placid, the lukewarm, the half-committed, the inconsistent, the paltry and mediocre. I long to avoid the selfish, the cheap, the shortcuts, the bargain price, the ultra-convenient, the easy, the quick and the accommodating.

I earnestly desire a Christianity that moves me off dead center; that flings me into the thick of the battle; that demands sacrifice and suffering; that tests my fiber; that causes me to weep over sin; that opens my mouth and engages my voice at the proper time. I want to have done with the shabbiness of sordidness, sadness, 'safety and slowness,' and self-sufficiency.

I want authentic Christianity...the kind that pulls down Jericho's walls; that walks on water; that raises the dead; that heals the sick and transforms the lost. I want a Christianity that puts me into the thick of the battle, that makes me different, and one that's worthy of the Name that is above all Names. I want a Christianity that brings a cross at the center of my walk, a gate at the end of my journey and a voice at the close of my pilgrimage that says, "WELL DONE."

Not Needed
in Heaven

When we get to heaven we will need no beauty aids because the church will be like a bride adorned for her husband. There will be no need for handkerchiefs or tissue because there will be no tears. No need for life insurance, burial policies, cemetery lots, or funeral homes, for death will be no more. There will be no need for physicians, hospitals, clinics, prescriptions, or aspirin, for the Bible says pain will be no more.

There will be no need of paint or repair tools because everything will be forever new. There will be no more water bills, for the Bible says we will be given the water of life from the fountain of life without payments.

There will be no need of laws, policemen, jails, courts or judges, for the Bible says that as for the cowardly, the faithless, the polluted, murderers, fornicators, sorcerers, idolaters, and all liars, their lot shall be in the lake that burns with fire. Since there will be no lawbreakers in heaven, there will be no need for a police force. There will be no Medicare, because the Bible says there will be trees there whose leaves are for the healing of the nations.

There will be no electric bills, for there will be no light bulbs, because there will be no night there; the Lord himself shall provide the light. There will be no food bills, no supermarkets, and no inflation. The Bible says the twelve fruit trees will be there yielding twelve kinds of fruit.

Finally, there will be no need of the gospel message there because all residents will be saved. I'm looking forward to that place, and trust that you are too!

RADICAL CHRISTIANITY

RADICAL CHRISTIANITY is a life-style, not just a mind-set; RADICAL CHRISTIANITY is concerned with conquering, not cowering; with sacrifice, not superficiality; with victory, not verbiage; with scoring, not slumming; with penetration, not pandering. RADICAL CHRISTIANITY is in first gear, neutral is nonexistent; RADICAL CHRISTIANITY is courageous but never constrictive, constraining or cautious! RADICAL CHRISTIANITY moves mountains; crosses Red Seas; pulls down walls; builds walls; walks on water; raises the dead; calms storms; feeds 5,000 and walks through closed doors.

It suffers regularly; soars often; sweats daily; saturates everything and spreads everywhere. RADICAL CHRISTIANITY calls sin black, hell hot, hypocrisy evil, Satan a liar and judgment sure. It doesn't back down, sit down or stay down. RADICAL CHRISTIANITY doesn't depend on the strokes of others to keep it going. It doesn't acquiesce in the face of loud opposition, fold under pressure, wince under criticism, tarnish under time, die under duress, fade under technology nor rot under moisture. It doesn't rust, retreat, renounce, reconsider, return nor renege. RADICAL CHRISTIANITY always lifts up Christ; knocks down barriers; marches over objections; overwhelms pessimism; gobbles up cynicism;

evaporates criticism; overcomes humanism; conquers defeatism and tramples down skepticism.

RADICAL CHRISTIANITY gives lavishly; prays relentlessly; claims abundantly; works feverishly; preaches powerfully; serves lovingly; perseveres patiently and believes expectantly! RADICAL CHRISTIANITY dares to challenge the prevailing standard to make it God's. It never plays to the grandstands; nor waters down its position; nor adjusts its principles, but rather is a thermostat that controls its surroundings, never a thermometer that merely adjusts to them. It is never big, popular, stylish, convenient, in vogue or in-step with the world. Its adherents are few; its sound clear; its philosophy unpopular and its rewards great. Its disciples aren't rewarded by this world but are those of whom Christ will say, "WELL DONE!"

THE REAL
VS. THE COUNTERFEIT

REAL Christianity never flinches at sacrifice; the counterfeit always looks for the bargain counter. REAL Christianity is concerned with giving; the counterfeit is only concerned with getting. REAL Christianity binds up dirty sores; the counterfeit passes by on the other side. REAL Christianity is built on conviction; the counterfeit is built on convenience. REAL Christianity proceeds by faith; the counterfeit goes by sight. REAL Christianity reaches out; the counterfeit always reaches in.

REAL Christianity goes for broke, while the counterfeit always plays it safe. REAL Christianity always bears a cross; the counterfeit just wears the crown. REAL Christianity loves in spite of; the counterfeits always love because of. REAL Christianity always dreams big dreams; the counterfeit never dreams at all. REAL Christianity lives on the battlefield; the counterfeit stays on the playground.

REAL Christianity follows Jesus regardless of the cost; the counterfeit follows what's popular and easy. REAL Christianity believes that faith can move mountains; the counterfeit tries to bulldoze them away. REAL Christianity spends its time in telling the Good

News; the counterfeit spends time watching the evening news. REAL Christianity makes disciples; the counterfeit just makes waves. REAL Christianity disturbs the comfortable; the counterfeit only comforts the disturbed. REAL Christianity pays the price and goes the distance; the counterfeit faces trials and runs. REAL Christianity builds character; the counterfeit just builds buildings. REAL Christianity never backs down; the counterfeit is in reverse most of the time. REAL Christianity is looking for Jesus to come; the counterfeit is just looking for retirement.

HURCH

Call it the company of the committed, the group of the gallant, the crew of the courageous, the fellowship of the faithful, or the battalion of the brave; the Church of Jesus Christ was never meant to be institutionalized. It was never meant to be an organization, but an organism; a living, breathing, pulsating, conquering outfit whose sole task is to change the world for Christ. Today, the "old ship of Zion" is scarred, bruised in spots, languishing in some quarters, but very much alive and still the number one threat to the kingdom of darkness. The Church cannot be destroyed, because the gates of hell cannot prevail against it. She's a stately lady who awaits the coming "Groom" to whisk her out of this world before the holocaust of God's wrath comes. The Church will emerge triumphant, victorious, and strong.

An Urgent Word
to the Church

O Church of God...get up and listen! Outside your walls a gasping world is hoarsely screaming for life! Wake up, O Church...shed your garments of convenience, your diluted gospel, your insipid spirit and your tame prophets. Strip yourself of sophistication, of dry eyes, unbent knees and business as usual. Recover, Church, the POWER, the PRESENCE, the PROMISE, the PASSION, the PURITY.

Hemorrhage, don't bleed; run, don't walk; shout, don't whisper; today, not tomorrow. Let your plans match my power, let your vision be unlimited, your dreams unleashed, your message uncompromising, your urgency undiluted, your prayers unfailing, your strategy unrelenting and your prophets unafraid!

Know your enemy, wear your armor, equip your saints, man your stations, give your dollars, show your colors, love your brother, hate all sin, preach my Gospel, DO IT NOW! Your clock is running out!

Divest yourselves of negative thinking, complaining talk, routine praying, constant shirking and hurt feelings. The time is short...very short...thus you cannot afford spectator membership, wishy-washy leadership, mediocre stewardship, narrow-cliquish fellowship or shoddy, thin discipleship! Peel away the tyranny of trivia, the pettiness of peevishness, the littleness of lovelessness, the blah of blurriness and the devil of divisiveness!

Remember who you are...my Bride...remember what you have...My power...remember who will win the battle...remember our slated rendezvous...I'm coming soon to get you, lady, I hope you're ready when I come.

Jesus

BRIDE OF CHRIST

This is the church - people not programs, power not promotion, penetrating, pulsating and populating the world with its gospel.

This is the church - battle scarred, often ravaged by the enemy, ignored by the lukewarm, passed over by the press, and ignored by the populace.

Yes, this is the church - a sleeping giant, potentially dangerous to a secular world, potentially victorious and potentially powerful.

This is the church - often shoved to the back burner, always put on hold, seldom taken seriously and usually not very visible. She stands, however, as a bulwark against the sordid and the filthy, against ungoliness and indifference, standing for holiness, righteousness, goodness and a world evangelized.

This is the church - opposing the devil and healing the sick, helping the poor, clothing the naked, feeding the hungry and saving the lost.

Its message may be misunderstood, its purpose may temporarily be buried, its power often unobserved, and its mission sometimes blurred. It's the only thing that will emerge in the end as victorious and triumphant. As God saved all who were in the ark, so God will save all who are in the church.

The church doesn't save, but is made up of the

saved. Jesus said the gates of hell will not prevail against her power and force. This is the church of the living Christ!

THE CHURCH'S DECLARATION TO SATAN

Satan, listen up, listen now, listen long and listen well! We're the Church of the Living God. We're bought with blood, charged with power, married to Jesus, indwelt with His Spirit, immune from destruction and destined for victory.

We won't fear your foolish foibles, run from your roaring, fold under your fire, be vulnerable to your vehemence, be scattered by your schemes, be derailed by your deceptions or lulled by your lies, buckle under your barking, acquiesce under your attacks, or be scared by your subtlety.

We're the company of the committed, the crowd of the covenant, the congregation of the courageous and a crew of the commissioned. We're the fellowship of the faithful, the battalion of believers, the regiment of the redeemed, the division of the devoted, the army of the approved, the team of the triumphant, the lot of the Lord's, the platoon of the powerful, and the vestige of the victorious.

We're not here to dread the war, plan the war, study the war, evaluate the war, or discuss the war. We came to win the war!

Satan, the clock is running out for you! We await

our rapture, but your rupture; our consummation, but your condemnation; our reign, but your ruin; our victory and your vindication; our success and your sorrow.

You can summon all your hosts, but you'll lose the battle! For He that is in us is greater than he that is in the world. We're the Church of the Living God! Blood-washed, spirit-filled, battle scared, unrelenting and indestructible. The gates of hell will not prevail against us.

Amen

DEAR WORLD

D ear World:
I am the Church...the Bride of
Christ...purchased by His blood and waiting
for His return. While I wait, however, you are my
concern, I care...I really do, I care that you hurt...that
you're lonely...that you are broken... bent... confused...
bewildered. I care that you're hungry...naked...
empty...insecure...directionless...and divided. I care that
you are duped by Satan, ruled by the spiritual hosts of
wickedness...tarnished by greed, made tired by
selfishness, scarred by the fall, raped by money-hungry
men, choking by the emission of man's "progress."

Oh, world my doors are open, my people waiting,
my Gospel powerful, my future bright, my plan
invincible, my Husband sovereign, my nature
indestructible... I am the Church! Kings have cursed
me, nations have beat me down...emperors have mocked
me... intellectuals have ignored me...rulers have scorned
me...crowds have passed me...but know this, when your
final convulsion comes, it will be MY people who stand
tall...victorious...serene. When evil belches up the
worst it has and tribulation covers every square inch of
your surface, my people will be taken up by my
Husband, who has never missed an appointment!

Dear World: leave your emptiness...your facade of
happiness...your appearance of well-being...your false

standards of having arrived...my doors are open...my terms the same...my offer good...my time limited. My groom will pardon your past, make meaningful your present and make hopeful your future. Your music box is winding down...your party almost over...your guests are weary...your decorations fading...your refreshments are running low...time is almost up. I'm waiting!

GREAT CHURCHES

A GREAT church pulsates with power, positiveness, prayer and persuasiveness. A GREAT church is a church whose leadership is on the cutting edge, whose vision is amazingly high, and mission is unmistakably clear. A GREAT church is never confused about its priorities. It is never held back by dwarfed planning and second-class happenings. A GREAT church is never content to 'get by.' It never chooses the cheapest way because it costs less, but always chooses the path that glorifies God, regardless of the cost.

GREAT churches are led by enthusiastic, visionary, selfless pastors who aren't afraid of work. GREAT churches don't just happen. They're built by the sovereignty of God and the work of people. GREAT churches have members that are not tippers, but tithers. GREAT churches have a burning desire to grow, plan to grow, strategize to grow, and organize to grow. GREAT churches never pull up and park by the victories of the past, but neither do they park by their failures. GREAT churches are not controlled by outward circumstances like recessions, locations, obstacles and climate, they forge ahead with big dreams and big plans, regardless of the environment.

GREAT churches thrive on meeting 'impossible' obstacles and roadblocks. GREAT churches are allergic to mundaneness, mediocrity, and maintaining. GREAT churches abandon reverse gear, neutral and park — the only gear that works is DRIVE! GREAT churches have a way of attracting GREAT people with GREAT generosity and GREAT commitment, people who share GREAT VISION for GREAT accomplishments.

LET'S HEAR IT FOR THE CHURCH

L et's hear it for the church...It is the bride of Christ and the body of Christ. It is the company of the saved, the champion of what is decent, pure, and clean in a dirty world.

Let's hear it for the church...The blood of the martyrs is still her seed. She has survived the innuendoes, the harassments, the criticisms.

She has been the brunt of jokes and sarcasm, she has been the recipient of barbs and accusations and can produce the scars from the beatings she has survived from her unthinking critics.

Let's hear it for the church...Created by Jesus, empowered by the Spirit, washed in the blood. Let her stand tall, unafraid, unashamed, unintimidated, and unapologetic.

Let's hear it for the church...For which Jesus died, often beat down, but not destroyed, scathed, but not diminished, cursed but not canceled, beat up, but not beat down.

Let's hear it for the church...Invincible, undying, victorious, steadfast, undefeated and ultimately the winner. Let her flag be unfurled, her message be magnified, her saints galvanized, her message recognized, and her enemies mesmerized.

Let's hear it for the church...And make ready for the risen, coming, redeeming Lord, who will rapture her away to glory and victory forever!

LIVE AND DEAD CHURCHES

D o you know the difference between LIVE churches and DEAD churches?

LIVE churches always have parking problems, dead churches don't.

LIVE churches are constantly changing methodology, dead churches don't have to.

LIVE churches have lots of "noisy" youth, dead churches are fairly quiet!

LIVE churches are constantly adding staff, dead churches usually have a surplus.

LIVE churches expenses always exceed their income, dead churches always take in more than they ever dream of spending.

LIVE churches are filled with folk with Bible in hand, dead churches aren't.

LIVE churches are intense and earnest about praise, dead churches aren't.

LIVE churches are constantly improving and planning for the future, dead churches worship their past.

LIVE churches grow so fast you forget people's names, in dead churches everybody knows everybody's name for years.

LIVE churches move out of faith, dead churches operate totally by sight.

LIVE churches support missions very heavily, dead churches keep it all at home.

LIVE churches focus on people, dead churches focus on program.

LIVE churches are filled with tithers, dead churches are filled with tippers.

LIVE churches dream great dreams for God, dead churches relive nightmares.

LIVE churches have the fresh wind of love blowing, dead churches are stale with bickering.

LIVE churches don't have "can't" in their vocabulary, dead churches have nothing else but.

LIVE churches evangelize! Dead churches fossilize.

NEEDED:
A FRESH VISITATION

Visit anew the Church, O God...purge her from timidity, tolerance, tiredness. Rib her saints with the steel of courage, commitment, compassion and color. Shore up the shallowness, the shyness, the sham, the sheepishness, the shakiness, the stuttering, the shiftiness, the shoddiness and the shrinkage. O Lord, mobilize her men, sterilize her convictions, stabilize her ship, cauterize her wounds, synchronize her strategy, fertilize her fields, pasteurize her life, revolutionize her loyalty and maxamize her message.

O God, help the Church to rid herself of the rummage, the residue, the rotten, the redundant, the ridiculous and the rubbish. Purify her preachers, multiply her millions, sanctify her saints, verify her message, magnify her gospel and stupefy her enemies. O God, let her troops pay any price, go any distance, suffer any loss, hurdle any obstacle, cross any river, climb any mountains, solve any problem, plumb any depths, ascend any heights, and cross any breadths to conquer this world for her mighty Groom.

O God, this is the Church. Let her have done with sight-walking, low living, empty talking, and tame plans. Lord, may the Church put on the coat of courage, the pants of power, the bonnet of boldness, the shirt of surety, the jacket of joy and the sandals of certainty.

Lord, trim the Church of the fat of folly, fickleness, fuzziness, and frailness, and teach her to flex her muscles with the power of the Holy Spirit. And Lord, before You come to get Your Bride, make sure she's stood tall, knelt low, lifted high and proclaimed broad. We await the visitation!

Normal Churches

Normal churches are melted together by the Spirit; subnormal churches are frozen together. Normal churches move by the Spirit; subnormal churches creep by committees. Normal churches do it now; subnormal just table the motion. Normal churches preach convulsively; subnormal churches lecture calmly. Normal churches double their budgets, subnormal churches double their meetings. Normal churches evangelize; subnormal churches fossilize. Normal churches hemorrhage; subnormal churches only bleed. Normal churches cross Red Seas on dry ground; subnormal churches jump mud puddles and get wet!

Normal churches are fishers of men; subnormal churches keep aquariums. Normal churches leap by faith; subnormal churches leap by limb. Normal churches multiply; subnormal churches only divide. Normal churches are run by God's power; subnormal churches manufacture their own. Normal churches go into orbit; subnormal churches stay on the launching pad. Normal churches shoot for the moon; subnormal churches try for the street light. Normal churches attempt the impossible; subnormal churches debate over the possible!

Normal churches will be raptured by Christ! Subnormal churches will be raptured by rot!

SAINT SKIPPING

This is the day of saint skipping in Evangelical Christianity. Saint skipping is a practice where Christians skip from one church to another in search of something different and new. Saint skippers usually never light. They attend awhile, do a personal evaluation of where they attend; but soon they travel on to another church. They seldom ever take part. Their only motive seems to be what they can get, not what they can give. In most cases, they tend to be hypercritical of programs and services, but seldom step forward and offer alternatives. Saint skippers are erratic in their giving. If they give at all, it is usually minimal. Their children seldom ever get involved in the youth or children's ministries...they aren't there long enough. Saint skippers are also elusive. They can attend a church, but because they never sign an attendance card or write a check, no one can show them concern or call them. This way they can say, "We attended that church for three months and no one ever called or came by."

Saint skipping is the art of avoiding responsibility and real discipleship. It is spiritual spectatorism at its height. Saint skippers are adept at coming, sitting, watching, criticizing, then going home...or to another performance to judge and evaluate. They become attendees of a dozen churches, but belong to none. They usually say they don't believe in organized religion. Yet, they are very organized in traveling from one place to another. Thank God for those who love the Lord, join a local church and perform their ministry there. These indeed are God's precious saints. If you know a saint skipper, encourage him or her to land, to light, to park, and to stay with a local body.

Stand Your Ground

STAND YOUR GROUND, O CHURCH! The enemy is on the rampage again...STAND YOUR GROUND! Let neither fear nor adversity daunt your mission! STAND YOUR GROUND! The cesspools of immorality and ungodliness are overflowing, but STAND YOUR GROUND!

The deceiving friends of lethargy and apathy have never been more present, but STAND YOUR GROUND! The godless cults are moving like a prairie fire to consume the immature, but, O CHURCH, STAND YOUR GROUND! Humanistic ideologies are running rampant to twist and warp the minds of our youth today, but STAND YOUR GROUND, O CHURCH. Satan's onslaught against marriage and the family is setting new records, but STAND YOUR GROUND!

Greed, lust, violence, murder, rape, perversion, drunkenness, pornography, lying, adultery and fraud are all having their day right now, but dear Church, STAND YOUR GROUND! Wolves in sheep's clothing have come within your gates and in some places stand within your pulpits, but, O CHURCH, STAND YOUR GROUND!

Much of your membership is at ease in Zion while many others are only playing church...but STAND YOUR GROUND, O CHURCH! The world system stands to oppose you, kings and governments legislate to limit you and most of the populace still ignores you, but STAND YOUR GROUND, DEAR CHURCH, STAND YOUR GROUND! O Church... remember who you are... a kingdom that cannot be shaken, a people to be reckoned with, a force that the gates of hell cannot hold back...an invincible army,...an indestructible organism that cannot be obliterated or detoured.

O Dear Church soon and very soon anti-Christs will appear to put the finishing touches to your demise, (or so they think), so...STAND YOUR GROUND! Hold high your head, remember your foundation. Keep ever before you, your ultimate destiny. And when the battle's done, the blood of your last martyr has dried, the noise of war has abated and the dust has settled, You, Dear Church, will stand! Scarred? Yes! Bruised? Weary? To be sure! But victorious and triumphant, you will stand, with sword drawn, your crown in place, and the enemy slain! So...here and now... in the midst of the battle, STAND YOUR GROUND, O CHURCH, STAND YOUR GROUND!

THE CHURCH'S CONFESSION

I am the Living Church! I was born in power. My birth is divine. Christ is my head. He bled for me. He died for me. He purchased me at the price of His life. The saved are harbored in me.

I've encountered the wrath of Rome, the curse of kings, the fire of fury, the sordidness of systems, the gore of governments. I've survived the turbulence of tyranny, the fleeting philosophies, the madness of monarchies, the poison of principalities, the attack of armies, the guns of giants and the darts of destruction.

I am invincible! I will not tolerate the insipidness of indifference or the atrophy of apathy; nor will I bless belated believing, placid plans, dwarfed dreams, insipid ideas or calm campaigns.

I am the Church; bought with blood, pulled by power, made to march, created to conquer, powered to proclaim, vowed to victory, delivered from deadness and lifted to life.

I am the Church; the living Church. Empires may oppose me, foes may reject me, the casual may ignore me, but I am destined for total victory, delivered from deadness, and lifted to life.

I am the Church; the living Church. My light may flicker, but never go out; my people may stagger, but never fall; my power be tested, but never overcome; my mission deferred but never deterred; my movement slowed but never stopped.

I am the Church of the living Christ. I will not be bought, compromised, altered, lost, done in or removed. I am the Church, and I am invincible!

THE CHURCH'S PRAYER FOR MILITANCY

O God, make us the church with unflinching loyalty, unswerving purpose, unadulterated truth! Let the church be ridiculously bold, hilariously generous, abnormally loving, incredibly compassionate but decidedly militant! Purge the church, O God, from blandness, blindness, blurriness and bleakness. Deliver her leaders from casualness, timidity, mediocrity, hypocrisy, hesitation and indecision.

Open her eyes, O God, to see the doors of hell being entered by millions weekly. Melt her paralysis, move her members, mold her plans, march her troops, mobilize her evangelists, maximize her power, mortify her fears and multiply her faith. O God, let the church have done with dwarfed plans, abbreviated dreams, sight-walking, trivia, bloodless preaching, insipid teaching, hollow meetings, sterile projects and meaningless maintenance.

Let the church catch the vision of the gospel's power, a changed world, gigantic faith and miracles performed! Let her members cross Red Seas on dry ground, march with faith around Jerichos and slay giants with slingshots. Increase her stride, enlarge her ranks, empower her plans, refine her message and recharge her faith. And when you come, Jesus, to get your Bride, may you find a stately lady, strong, battle-scarred, unbent, unafraid, unashamed, untarnished, unbeaten, uncompromising, undaunted...ready for her Lord. Give her now the vision of the strategy settled, the battle done, the victory won, the issue settled and the church triumphant!

Amen

THE CHURCH'S PRIORITY PRAYER

God, I am the church! Purge me from impotency... rid me of casualness, strip me of pseudo-sophistication; peel away my preoccupation with status quo...knock away my false props of popularity and promotion...tear away the tyranny of trivia and burn away the chaff of compromise...scrape from my life the rust of resistance, the tired traditions, the meaningless meetings and hollow cliches. Prep me for battle, fill me with power, arm me with courage, show me the enemy, compel me to go!

I am the church! Redeem me from being a recluse, point me to purpose, raise up my vision and show me the victory. Let me not muddle in the mundane, rest on past victories, dilute my message, or make smaller my boundaries. Make my gospel clear, my target sure, my timing right and my motive pure.

Clear my agenda of all that is small, temporary, mediocre, humanly attainable, comfortable and consistent with the world...I am the church. May my members be unflinching in conviction, liberal in giving, non-retreating and courageous... let them pay the price, run the distance, suffer the loss, bear the shame and win the battle.

I am the Church of God! When the carriage comes at the close of the age to take me home, let me be a stable lady to meet my groom. May my scars be from battle, not blunders; my crown be from heaven, not earth; my coronation from Christ, not man. I am the Church! Let me never forget that when the dust and heat of the battle have settled, I will stand invincible, victorious and triumphant.

Amen.

WHAT KIND OF CHURCH WILL IT TAKE?

A confused, chaotic, convulsing world gasping for life and breath will not be touched by a tame church, mouthing time-worn clichés and pious platitudes. To take the world for Christ demands a church Spirit-filled, Spirit-led, Spirit-directed, Spirit-drenched, Spirit-powered, and Spirit-moved. It will take a visionary church, unafraid of gigantic dreams and audacious plans. A church convicted, compassionate, committed, compelled, and courageous.

To affect a dirty world, it will take a pure church. To rapture an apathetic world it will take a convicted church. To affect a sad world it will take a happy church. To challenge a dying world, it will take a living church. To heal a sick world, it will take a well church.

It will take a church unafraid of danger, unaffected by roadblocks, unflinching in the face of criticism, and unmoved by persecution. It will take a church that dares to dream big, to work long, to pray desperately, to plan carefully, to fight bravely, to storm the gates of evil and lethargy. It will take a church that is unwilling to compromise, willing to sacrifice, ready to be inconvenienced, and more than eager to risk. It will take a church committed to conquering, available for advance, always daring to detonate the destructive dynamite of the devil.

It will take a church whose strength is equal to her task, a church claiming all the gifts of the Spirit, all the power available, and all the authority given. It will take a church with Godly gusto, victorious venture, prevailing prayer, and demonstrative determination to win the battle.

It will take a church blood-washed, Spirit-filled, divinely sent, moving, planning, risking, and conquering with supernatural power.

WHICH CHURCH RAPTURED?

I am just about ready to come for you, my beloved, my Church! I do hope you are READY! I've been gone 2,000 years, and I've wondered if I'll still recognize you...but then, of course, I know I will. You have certain marks that say you are unmistakably mine. The Church I'm coming to get is a Church untarnished by sin, unblemished by faithlessness, unsoiled by cowardice.

I will recognize it when I come because it will be a church aggressively pursuing the world with My gospel, making big plans, conquering new frontiers, blazing new trails and not counting the cost. It will be the Church free of mediocrity, mundaneness and muddled priorities. It will be the loving Church, the living Church, the learning Church, the longing Church and the lilting Church.

It will be a Church with vision high, sin low, work long, prayer deep, giving broad, and love wide. It will be the Church that has taken the great commission seriously, the one that pays any price, hurdles any barrier, suffers any inconvenience to see that the gospel is preached. It will be the Church whose members really pay a price to belong; a church filled with workers and doers, not sitters and spectators.

Yes, I'm coming for My Church. I'll know her by her battle scars, her faithful pastors and leaders, the number of disciples she has produced and the number of missionaries she has sent. I'm coming soon...I do hope you're ready.

Jesus

 OMMITMENT

Namby-pamby, halfhearted, lethargic, and watered down promises are a dime a dozen. Contracts are broken in the time it takes to blink an eye, people go back on their word, and promises aren't followed through much anymore. God is still looking for people today whose hearts are totally committed to Him. No wavering, no detouring, no washouts, no excuses...just plain old commitment. When you say, "Jesus is Lord!" it means He is Lord! If He is Lord, I'm His servant and have lost the right to run my own show and set my own agenda. When the U.S. Marine Corps used to advertise, "We need a few good men," they weren't looking for wimps, but for people who stood by their word and would do what they promised. We need to put this commodity of commitment back on the shelves again today.

A KINGDOM PERSON

A Kingdom person is someone arrested by the King. He's sold out, lock, stock and barrel to Kingdom issues! He's moved by Kingdom causes...he dances to Kingdom music...he's thrilled with Kingdom victories...he loves Kingdom subjects...he's committed to Kingdom agendas...he stands for Kingdom standards...he follows Kingdom orders...he preaches the Kingdom gospel...he invests in Kingdom enterprises...he's on a Kingdom schedule...he engages in Kingdom conversation...and holds to a Kingdom value system...he's in the Kingdom army...he knows the Kingdom's Book...he speaks the Kingdom's language...he fulfills the Kingdom's purpose...he gives lavishly to Kingdom projects...he enjoys the Kingdom's blessings...he fights the Kingdom's battles...he achieves by Kingdom power...he defends Kingdom positions...he endorses Kingdom conquests...he worships the Kingdom's King...he cheers the Kingdom's efforts...he mourns the Kingdom's losses...he pays the price for Kingdom membership...and if need be,...he dies for the Kingdom's honor!

Is it any wonder that the Bible says: "...We are receiving a kingdom that cannot be shaken!"

(Hebrews 12:28)

A Prayer

L ord,

I'm willing to receive what you give,

To relinquish what you take,

To suffer what you allow,

To be what you require,

To do as you command.

A Prayer for Purity

R evisit, O God, Your servant...let the flame of Pentecostal FIRE singe the frayed edges of my sinfulness...like polluted water boiled clean, so boil my tarnished spirit in cleansing fire! Breathe holiness on my soiled and sullied attitudes...With high and toxic explosives.

O God, blow apart my pride and arrogance, with intense and destructive heat, burn out of my life the alloy of apathy, the sham of shoddiness, the rottenness of rudeness, the poison and pus of pretentiousness, the filth of foolishness, the acid of assertiveness, the heinousness of hypocrisy, the darkness of doubt, the moldiness of mediocrity, and the staleness of stubbornness!

Burn...fire of God, burn, cauterize the impurity of my thoughts, the vested interests of my decisions, the selfishness of my actions, the carelessness of my tongue, the forbidden things of my eyes, and the wrong direction of my feet. I so desperately need your fire, O God...to warm an oft cold heart, to lighten an oft dark path, to consume excessive slash, to make crisp, limp and lazy attitudes. Let the flame that burned at Pentecost burn above my head, before my path, within my heart, throughout my mind, upon my tongue, on my lips, and beneath my feet till I am claimed, cleansed, commissioned, and conquering! And when the burning is over let me appear before you as pure gold, free from alloy!

I hereby relinquish all rights, all say so, all privileges Lord! I'm sold out to You! Preach through my lips, praise through my tongue, heal through my hands, see through my eyes, and hear through my ears. Let your mark of ownership be visible for all to see. Shake me, break me, take me, and make me in Your image. I'm Your slave and wait for Your bidding.

Amen

A Prayer
for Today

Lord, today is here! It came so fast! Before my feet hit the floor prepare me for it. A whole menagerie of things await me. . . problems, pressures, pitfalls, pain and perils...make my skin tough Lord, to bear it all. I may be lied to, laughed at, looked down upon, lurched or left. I may be deceived and discriminated against, but help me respond in love; I may be praised and complimented, Lord, make me humble; I may be cheated today, overcharged or had, insulted, condemned or criticized, but help me not to be vindictive.

My patience will be tested, my calmness shattered, my tranquillity punctured and my vision blurred, but in the pace of it all Lord, let me keep my perspective. All kinds of people will cross my path today Lord, little people, stingy people, angry people, loving people, impatient people, hurt people, hypocritical people, mean people, nice people, kind people, lovely people...all kinds, but regardless of who they are, may they see Christ in my response.

This is your day Lord, cover me with the insulation of Your presence, the warmth of Your love, the surety of Your direction, and the power of Your sovereignty. Lord, the day is here, prepare me for it. Make me ready for the inconveniences, the waits, the detours, the interruptions, the red lights and the unexpected. This is Your day, You have made it Lord, I will rejoice and be glad in it.

A Prayer for Zeal

Lord, get me off dead center! Wind my clock, get me up, get me out, get me moving...the world is burning down...time is running out...I must get up! Let me catch the urgency, feel the compulsion, sense the limited time and get on with what you want to do with me. Lord, operate on me! Remove the lethargy, the laziness, the lulling laxness and lingering, and lift me to limitless tasks for you! O Lord, where I hide, find me; where I drag, propel me; where I postpone, discipline me; where I meander, motivate me. O Lord, don't allow me to become another waiter, watcher, whistler or whiner, but by your prodding, make me a mover of men and promoter of visions. Take Your fire, O God, and purge out of my system all the debris that clogs my life and keeps me waterlogged.

Amen

A PRAYER TO BE SPIRIT FILLED

Spirit of God, fill me today. Strip me of pride and pretense...scrub me clean of all the dirt of doubt, dullness, drabness and dryness! Brand me with the branding iron of ownership with a burn so deep, the scar will go into eternity. Holy Spirit boil out of my spirit the encrustment of deadness, diluted do-nothingness, dreariness and decrepitude.

Oh, Spirit, bleach my mind, drench the heat of my temper, cauterize the poison of my tongue, scrape off the barnacles of brashness, boastfulness and bullishness. Oh, Spirit, burn out of me all the alloy, all the impurity, all the defects, all the self, the sordidness, the surliness, the sarcasm, and all the sundry sins that sear my spirit!

Spirit of God, move in, knock down, sweep out, refurnish, refurbish, redecorate, readorn, recreate, restore, renew, revise, reschedule, repossess, recommission, revive, reveal!

Consume, Oh Spirit, any vestige of indifference, infidelity, insubordination, inordinateness, ineptness, intemperance, incongruity, inconsistency, incredulity, indolence and indulgence. Keep my eyes fixed, my ears open, my tongue loving, my feet ready, and my hands willing. Electrify me with joy, endue me with boldness, clothe me with concern, permeate me with pulsating power.

Don't make me comfortable, but committed, don't give me rest, but revival until every waking moment I am aware that I am possessed by an alien power and presence.

Holy Spirit, arrest me now, I turn the title deed of my life over to you! Empty me of me...fill me with You, plug up the leaks and ready me for the spiritual warfare that's already here!

AN URGENT PRAYER

Dear Lord,
I'm a servant of Yours. I have been won to witness, not just watch, saved to serve, not just sing. Wash me from all the debris and dinginess of drab duty, O God, and get me off the dime. Shake me 'til all the junk collected from casual living falls off. Rid me of all stinkin' thinkin', do-nothingness, and the so-what attitude. Break my pride, bend my knees, loosen my tongue, lift my hands, stir my spirit, and prepare my hands for work.

Make me a blazing torch, O God. Burn from my life all the dross, all the residue, and the redundant. Purge me of all that is putrid and paltry, and rib me with the steel of courage that is contagious.

Lord, I offer myself to You anew today. Take me, break me, remake me to be used for Your utmost. In a world of ease and lethargy, let me hemorrhage for You, O Lord, until the whole world knows the Gospel.

Amen

At His Disposal

Lord, I'm totally at Your disposal, use me for what You will. Lord, I'm a furnace, burn within me...I'm a letter, mail me any place You like; I'm a scythe, use me to harvest whomever and whenever...I'm an arrow, aim me and shoot me anyplace You like; I'm oil, pour me on the wounds of a hurting world; I'm a rocket, launch me to your destination. I'm a missile, use me to be a target or hit a target for You.

Lord, I'm a car, drive me as far as and as long as You like to wherever You desire; I'm a rake, drag me across a dirty world and use my tongs to gather up undesirable debris; I'm an ear, Lord, use me to hear the hurt and heartache of lonely, suffering people. Lord, I'm a bandage, stick me on all the owies, scratches, bruises, cuts, lacerations of humanity. I'm a bell, Lord, ring me as long and as loud as You like; I'm a bridge, use me to connect broken relationships, I'm a socket, plug into me anything You want to run.

Lord, I'm a knife, sharpen my blade to cut out of my life all that is rotten and unproductive; I'm a hammer, weld me and break into pieces my prejudices, my arrogance, and my selfishness; I'm elastic, Lord, stretch me around anyone, anything, anytime in anyway to hold together any situation that is falling apart; I'm a shovel, Lord, dig with me till every 'root of bitterness' is gone; I'm a magnet, Lord, draw with me any and all who are weak and heavy-laden. I'm a cup, fill me or empty me, store me or display me, but use me for Your highest.

Lord, I'm a computer, feed into me all that You want retained; I'm a disposal, pour down my drain all that You want destroyed; Lord, I'm a broom, use me to sweep clean a world littered with dirt; I'm an eraser, rub me across the errors of our time; I'm a microphone, speak into me that which You want amplified for all the world to hear. Lord, I'm a tire, roll me over whatever surface You desire for as long as You wish; Lord, I'm a rag, apply Your hand to me to clean up the grease and grime of my civilization; I'm a tent, Lord, use me to cover whoever for as long-ever for any reason! Lord, I'm a fire, use me to warm people, to burn out alloy, or provide energy. Lord, I'm a pencil, use me to write Your message to the world; I'm Yours Lord, I'm totally at Your disposal.

Amen

My Public Declaration

I 've caught the vision, made the decision, stepped over the line; the die has been cast, the step has been taken, the confession has been made, the promise has been spoken, I have become a follower of Jesus Christ! My past is redeemed, my present secured, my future made hopeful, my bridges have been burned, my old life crucified, my new life sanctified, the journey begun, the goal is from sight to faith, from guilt to wholeness, from darkness to light, from prison to freedom, I'm on my way!

Nothing will deter me, drag me, deceive me, detour me, derail me, deprive me, de-program me or destroy me...I won't look back, turn around, slow down, fall down, or go down. I've entered the race; full of power, delivered from weakness; full of hope, delivered from despair; full of faith, delivered from doubt; full of courage, delivered from Satan; and full of boldness. Obstacles won't tire me; pleasures won't allure me; for I've made the choice, settled the account, sealed the orders, filed the flight plan, and am on my way. I'm done with low vision, sight-walking, mini-dreaming, meaningless meandering, dwarfed doings, petty projects and cheap talk. I'm through with halfhearted commitment, mediocrity, broken promises and shoddy discipline. With a new mind, I'll think holy thoughts; with a new tongue, I'll speak a new message; with a new walk, I'll go different places; with new eyes, I'll see different visions. I've been bought with a price, sealed with His Spirit and guaranteed an inheritance. From this day forth, I'll live like a prince coming into his inheritance.

PRAYER OF COMMITMENT

God, forgive me for conducting "business as usual." Purge me of bland, insipid worship. Save me from casual evangelism. Moisten the dryness of my eyes at the sight of a lost world. Strip me of pride and boastfulness. Transform smoldering sparks into unquenchable blazes. Deliver me from shoddy commitments and cheap involvement. Sicken me of trifling with trivia and promoting a proliferation of prayerless programs. Rescue me from the redundancy of rhetoric and show me that the kingdom does not consist of talk but of power.

Snatch me from the tyranny of the important and pre-occupy me with the essential. Replace fearful caution with boldness, sight-walking with faith-living, dwarfed-dreams with giant visions, and reluctance with reliance.

Salvage me from the subtlety of sidestepping my mission, redeem me from low vision, high-mindedness, shallow thinking. Dislodge me, O God, from the deadly deception of spectator religion. Grant me eyes to see a lost world, ears to hear the cry of hurting people, hands to lift, feet to run to humanity in need and arms to lift the lonely and lost.

Reduce me to repentance. Drive me to my knees, remind me again and again of who's boss. Make me electric with excitement, verbal in witness, extravagant in giving, and liberal in love. Above all, O God, bind me to the Book, that from it I may grow to be a daring disciple.

Amen.

PRAYER OF POSSESSION

God, I don't want to possess You, I want You to possess me. Strip me, Lord, of all the spiritual junk I've accumulated that isn't conducive to Your cause. Peel away from my life, O Lord, layers of meaningless tradition, of unproductive habits, of all that is ungodly and unfitting. Clear from my agenda O Lord, all that is mundane and meaningless, and replace it with divine appointments. Clear my calendar Lord, of any and all appointments that won't enhance Your Kingdom, further Your gospel, or glorify Your Name.

O Lord, I want my schedule to be planned by You. Remove from my mind all that is low, lewd, lethargic and limiting, and recharge my energy with power that is divine. O Lord, I stand before You today in neutral, asking that You shift me into high, low, reverse or park. Put Your hand on the wheel; turn me left or right. Place Your hand upon my eyes and cause me to see the need close at hand or far away. I'm Yours, O Lord, and I relinquish the title deed of my life anew, and welcome You as the new Owner and Operator.

Amen

QUALIFICATIONS FOR A DISCIPLE

WANTED: Disciples. Hours will be 168 per week; pay is zero. No experience required, but toughness and resiliency helpful. No retirement provided in this life, but unlimited benefits in the next! Working conditions aren't the best. There are hassles, discrimination, put-downs, and even persecutions

In this job, it's mostly give and no take. There are few breaks, no vacations, no sick leave, no material bonuses, few, if any, compliments and only one promotion which comes at the end of your life.

Applicants must be willing to sacrifice, study long, pray hard, labor unceasingly, and must be willing to be called a "fool" for Christ's sake. The job is not easy. You will often work alone, but you will never be alone. People in this line of work are in a minority. Applicants must be willing to share their testimony in crowds that are both sympathetic and antagonistic; both understanding and prejudiced.

Applicants must realize that identification with our organization makes them unpopular with the majority. Applicants must be prepared to live any place on earth. All applicants are required to understand, before they sign up, that they must relinquish all rights, legal or otherwise, to all personal property such as cars, houses, real estate, money, recreational vehicles, stocks, IRA account; in fact, EVERYTHING.

Applicants are urged to consider strongly their decision to come on board since our policy is there is no getting out once in! Our policy is clear, "No one who puts his hand to the plow and looks back is fit for the Kingdom of God."

Though this position is hazardous, there are great rewards and satisfaction to the work. We believe that "in due season we shall reap if we don't faint."

Those interested may apply at the foot of the cross! There is no legal age limitation and whosoever will, may come.

THE LORD'S WORD TO A BELIEVER

Hey, believer, it's not time for placid calmness. It's a time to go for broke for Me. It's a time to move, not meander; to march, not mutter; a time to man the ship, not mute the lip.

I want the knee bent, the Word sent, the gospel preached, the world reached, the sinner lured, the saint matured, sin forsaken, the message taken, the Bible read, the hungry fed. I want the lost reclaimed with the preacher inflamed!

O believer, the time is short...don't table any motions...or defer any decisions...shed the mundane, abandon the mediocre, skip over the preface, get to the point, avoid the peripheral, preach hell hot, sin black, the Bible true, and Jesus coming again. Tell my Bride to stand tall, kneel often, run fast, reach far, give freely, be victorious, love abundantly, preach ferociously, and wait patiently.

It's not a time to plan, but a time to proceed; not a time to meet, but a time to march; not a time to appraise, but a time to attack; not a time to read the minutes, but to pass the motions; not a time for neutral, but a time for drive.

THE WIND OF REVIVAL

Blow...blow...blow...wind of the Spirit, like a mighty gale, across Your Church right now! Blow away her sin, her shame, the dirt of degeneracy, blow away the lingering vestiges of luke-warmness and laxity, or 'business-as-usual' attitude, our stale and sterile stupor...blow, wind of the Spirit and scatter our proneness to perpetually ponder, putter, play and preoccupy ourselves only with the peripheral!

Holy Spirit of God, as on Pentecost, let the rushing roar of Your mighty wind dissipate our do-nothingness and deadness, our dreariness! With hurricane force, sweep away any and every tradition that is trite, every plan that is paltry, every idol we've exalted and every boast that's benign. With tornado velocity, let Your wind, O Spirit, rip up and sail away all that clutters Your Church, the rubble, the rancid, the recalcitrant, the repulsive, the rusty and routine.

Blow...wind of the Spirit, across our dry bones, connect them together, then through Your freshness, fill us with life! Blow hard, O Spirit, till all that isn't nailed down comes up and is removed. Then like a cool, refreshing breeze, gently blow across Your Church the spirit of revival, prayer, repentance, consecration, commitment, resolve, worship, praise and glory.

Amen

WAIT-WATCHERS

Evangelical Christianity is fighting a plague WITHIN its ranks. It is one of Satan's most subtle deceptions. The plague is incarnate in a group of people known as WAIT-WATCHERS. WAIT-WATCHERS do what their name implies, they WAIT and WATCH! They have been known to be drifters... drifting from one church to another, WAITING, then WATCHING, then moving on to another "performance." There is an aloofness about them...in fact some are artists at "slipping" in and out without being detected, thus giving no opportunity for any church to pay them a visit, for that might mean involvement.

These WAIT-WATCHERS sometimes find a church they like, but they wait, wait, and wait before joining, because they never seem to be through with WATCHING. They never seem to "light" but continue to "fly" from church to church. They are detached and like it that way. They are somehow "above" settling down and being a participating member of a local church. They are high on attending, but invisible in involvement.

As a rule, WAIT-WATCHERS give little or nothing in the offering. Why should they? They really aren't a part of the ministry of that local church, so why pay? They're really hard to distinguish from the others, you'll always see them in the worship service porking down the food of the Word, but you WON'T see them ushering, directing traffic in the parking lot, teaching a class, helping in the nursery, greeting at the door, or driving the bus, it's not their "thing."

WAIT-WATCHERS are never criticized by anyone (except me!) because they never do anything. They come, sit, WAIT, WATCH, listen, then go home till next performance. I really pity these people because they're missing the joy of the Lord! I trust you aren't a WAIT-WATCHER! In these last days, God is calling for soldiers, uniformed, armed, marching and moving for Him. It's that army Jesus is coming to rapture someday. Praise God!

WHAT TIME IS IT?

It's time to man the ranks...to identify the enemy...to clarify the strategy. It's a time to fight, not fidget; a time to act, not acquiesce; a time to be bold, not bland; a time to march, not meander; a time to give and not groan; a time to conquer, not cower; a time to press on, not panic out; a time to soar, not sink; a time to surge, not snore; a time to heed, not hedge; a time to change, not churn; it's definitely a time to forge ahead, not fiddle around!!

It's time to crucify self, to nullify sin, to verify truth, to sanctify saints; it's a time to detour trivia, a time to leap, not jump; a time to spring, not jog; a time to dispense with the reading of the minutes, dismiss the meeting, and speed to the fire. It's a time of urgency that demands action. It is a time to do more praying than planning; a time to wear out shoes instead of lead in pencils; a time for more exclamation points than commas; a time for more gears in first than neutral.

ONVICTIONS

Convictions: Who has them anymore? Who wants them? Who needs them? Sound familiar? Sure it does. We live in a day of "relativity." Boards of surety we thought were nailed down securely are coming up today. Many seem to be "waffling" and caving in to compromise and convenience. We need a new breed of men and women who will be committed to old fashioned, Bible centered, convictions. Some things don't change. Two plus two equaled four in 1675. Guess what? Two plus two still euqls four! God is God, the Bible is true, the Gospel is sure, and Jesus is definitely coming again. These things don't change; only we change! We need a fresh anointing of old-fashioned CONVICTIONS today! We must stand for something or we will fall for anything!

A PREACHER'S PRAYER

O God...don't let the pulpit call me to the sermon...let the sermon call me to the pulpit. Before I break the bread of life, Lord, break me! Wash from heart and lip the iniquity there...I want to preach under the divine anointing. God...strip me of all pride...all cleverness...all showmanship...and salesmanship. Deliver me from reliance on suaveness, education, academics, personality, notes, canned quips, and celestial clichés. Let me speak with the humility of Moses, the patience of Job, the wisdom of Paul, the power of Peter, and the authority of Christ. Lord, make my preaching clear, not clever; passionate, not pitiful; urgent, not 'usual'; meaty, not murky. May it comfort the disturbed, disturb the comfortable, warn the sinner, mature the saint, give hope to the discouraged, and ready for Heaven the whole audience.

Let self be abased, Christ be exalted, the Cross be central and the plea be with passion. May my eyes never be dry. Just now, Lord take me out of myself, usurp anything I've planned to say when it's in the way of YOUR message. Here I am, Lord, I'm your vessel!

Amen

A TIME TO MOVE

This is an urgent time for the militant church! It is a time to forge, not fumble! It is a time to lunge ahead, not linger, to be ready for revival, not a time to back away!

It is a time to fly, not flounder, to expect miracles, not mundaneness...to dress for war, not waltzing...to be victors, not victims...to proclaim...not procrastinate!

It is a time for the Church to stand tall, speak authoritatively, rebuke Satan, walk on water, go for broke and hold God to His Word! It is not a time to speculate, postulate, castigate, hallucinate, or calculate, but rather a time to instigate, elucidate, germinate, and propagate the Gospel as never before!

Get up, O Church, scrape the rust and barnacles off, and hurl yourself into the fight. The time is short, the need urgent, workers few but God is adequate!!! It's time for revival, so let it begin with me!

By Faith or Sight

Faith-walking moves, then asks; sight-walking asks, then moves; faith-walking trusts, sight-walking looks; faith-walking proceeds before the facts are in, sight-walking busily gathers facts and considers; faith-walking believes God, sight-walking believes only what it sees; faith-walking is directed by divine light, sight-walking sees by flashlight; faith-walking conquers, sight-walking only considers; faith-walking runs up mileage, sight-walking is measured in feet and inches.

Faith-walking excites the walker, sight-walking only exhausts; faith-walking wins victories, sight-walking makes victims; faith-walking moves mountains, sight-walking examines molehills; faith-walking lunges ahead, sight-walking cautiously shuffles along; faith-walking thrives on obstacles, sight-walking is stopped by them; faith-walking soars in the supernatural, sight-walking nestles into the natural; faith-walking confidently crosses Red Seas and Jordan Rivers, sight-walking struggles in ankle-deep mud puddles.

Faith-walking explores the unknown, sight-walking studies the familiar; faith-walking trusts where it cannot see, sight-walking sees where it cannot trust; faith-walking conquers, sight-walking only covers; faith-walking is an adventure, sight-walking is only a bad trip; faith-walking is God's way, sight-walking is man's way; faith-walking takes you to heaven, sight-walking takes you elsewhere.

God, Give Me Courage!

G od, give me courage...courage to stand, to speak, to go the distance, pay the price, take the risk, and take the flack! Give me courage to live by truth instead of what's easy, to place principle above popularity, conviction above convenience, and right above recognition.

God, give me courage to be confident in the face of criticism, brave in the midst of barrage, assured in the onslaught of attack, dedicated at the time of decision, and focused in the moment of fire; give me courage to say no when all others are saying yes; courage to follow when the majority scatters; courage to keep marching when the rest are meandering; courage to go when the crowd says stay; courage to walk when others just talk; courage to hope when many just cope; courage to contend when others pretend; courage to shout when most just doubt; courage to stay the course, hold the line, finish the race, complete the journey, and never cave in.

God, give me courage to be the maverick, set the pace, carry the torch, be called the fool, be laughed at, scorned, ridiculed, hated, written off, abused, or ignored, but let that courage keep me at my post, lifting high Your truth, Your standard, Your word, and Your promise! Give me courage to not jump ship, bail out, run away, be intimidated, forsake the call, cave in, compromise, or cow-tow, or run.

God, give me courage to dream big dreams, see large visions, plow new ground, chart new courses, sail new seas, and set new records. Give me courage to put character above compromise, purity above the popular, resolve above what's applicable, passion above pleasure, faithfulness above flippancy!

God, give me courage to think Your thoughts, obey Your commands, follow Your path, take the guff, suffer the loss, carry Your cross, and be Your faithful disciple, clear to the end.

Amen

MAKE A DECISION

Lord, clear the blurred lines out of my life. Cleanse me from gray areas. Remove from my vocabulary words like "sort of" and "kind of" and "somewhat." Let yes be yes, and no be no. Help me to stand for You, lest I fall for anything. Purge me from sidestepping, from excuse making, from double-talk, from shifting standards, from adjustable morals. Never allow my silence to be a cop-out. Let me speak, walk, hear, see, and live so the world will never have to guess where I stand with You.

Amen

Satan's Travel Agency

THE GUILT TRIP: Christians sin — I John 2 even tells us that when we do, we have an advocate with the Father, Jesus Christ. But Satan has been successful in convincing some Christians that if they sin, there's no more hope for them. He's convinced them that God's grace covered only their past sins when they accepted Christ. The old guilt trip makes you feel depressed, defeated and deflated. It causes you to drop out of things, leave the Christian fellowship and ultimately die spiritually unless Satan's trick can be exposed.

THE FEELING TRIP: Satan knows if he can make Christians dissatisfied with their spiritual level, he can make them seek some kind of "second blessing" or some ecstatic "experience" or "tongue" or "vision." He has even been successful in convincing believers who haven't had that "extra icing" that they are inferior. They are coaxed to "seek a gift" so they can be on a higher plane. The feeling trip causes the believer to base his whole faith on a "good feeling." A modern song's lyrics say, "It can't be wrong when it FEELS so right..." This places the reality or unreality of one's faith on the level of feeling instead of faith and fact. We must remember however that one's experience never substantiates the Word of God...rather the Word of God must substantiate someone's experience. This feeling trip sets Christians back, not forward; Beware!!

THE COMPROMISE TRIP: Satan loves this trip because it does permanent Kingdom damage. This is the trip that convinces truly born-again people that there really is no conflict with being a Christian and being immoral. Examples? Some churches across our land see no conflict with being Christian and being "gay." A book has been written by a "Christian" homosexual, *The Lord Is My Shepherd and He Knows That I'm Gay.* Can you fathom that?

Want another example? There are thousands of so called "Christians" who come to church every Sunday, but who live together without the benefit of marriage, all in the name of LOVE. Satan loves this trip and would like to take you on it so that increasingly you can endorse the lurid and the unseemly. He starts by getting you to "tolerate" it. Toleration gives way to endorsement. God forbid that we take this trip. It leads to spiritual disaster.

THE COP-OUT TRIP: Many Christians have already booked passage on this one! It's the trip that refuses to allow the believer to assume any responsibility in the church because he is "being fed." It's the trip that justified a Christian's refusal to accept a job or ministry in the body because he wants to get built up spiritually first.

Now we all know that spiritual feeding is a must. Many have been burned out working at too many tasks without adequate spiritual re-enforcement... but we also know "if the intake exceeds the output, the upkeep will be the downfall."

If you need to take a trip, go to Hawaii or Florida. Pass up Satan's' travel agency. His tickets are all one-way!!!

THIS IS WHERE I STAND

I'm a sin-hating, devil-stomping, demon-conquering, hell-avoiding, fully-forgiven, blood-washed, Spirit-filled, Bible-believing, church-attending, praise-producing, sanctified, witnessing, loving, tithing, serving, excited child of the living God.

I hate the devil, immorality, lying, humanism, compromise, abortion, homosexuality, fornication, adultery, apathy, gossip, prostitution, laziness, and deadness in churches.

I love the Lord, His Book, His Son, His Church, His Gospel, the Blood, holiness, the brethren, worship, praise, evangelism, the Holy Spirit, purity, the offering, and revival.

I look forward to a world won, the devil defeated, the press truthful, politicians saved, the oppresed delivered, the government frugal, prayer in public schools, the rapture of the church, the final judgement, and reigning with Christ in a new body!

I'm consumed with going, working, sharing, telling, persuading, convincing, praying, sowing, reaping, producing, winning and discipling the whole world to Jesus Christ.

# DISCIPLESHIP

The word DISCIPLE means a "learner." A learner is one who follows his teacher around, and becomes like that teacher. When you accepted Jesus Christ, you got so much; forgiveness of sin, eternal life, the Holy Spirit, abundant life, etc. The Lord got you! What did He get? Hopefully, one who is willing to follow when it's convenient and when it's not...one who's willing to be sold out when it's free and when it's costly...one who is willing to be totally devoted to obedience when it's easy and when it's hard. Discipleship is FOLLOWship! It's saying, in the words of that old hymn, "Where he leads me I will follow." It speaks in words of loyalty, availability, devotion, and commitment. It pays the price, goes the distance, stays the course, suffers the loss, and bears a cross. It never looks back once the hand is on the plow. When the question is asked, "Am I a fully-devoted follower of Jesus Christ?" it always answers YES.

Fellowship of The Unashamed

I am part of the Fellowship of the Unashamed. I have Holy Spirit power. The dye has been cast. I have stepped over the line, the decision has been made...I am a disciple of Jesus, I won't look back, go back, hold back, let up, slow down, back away, hesitate or be still! My past is redeemed, my present remade and my future re-aimed. I am finished and done with low living, sight walking, small planning, smooth knees, colorless dreams, tame visions, mundane talking, chintzy giving, dwarfed goals, deficient faith and cheap grace.

I no longer need preeminence, prosperity, position, promotions, plaudits, prestige or popularity. I don't have to be right, first, tops, recognized, praised, regarded, or rewarded. I now live by presence, lean by faith, love by patience, lift by prayer and labor by power.

My face is set, my gait is fast, my goal is Heaven, my gift is grace and my God is good...my road is narrow, my way is rough, my companions few, my guide reliable, my mission clear and my power sufficient. I cannot be bought, compromised, detoured, lured away, turned back, diluted, distracted, deterred or delayed. I will not flinch in the face of sacrifice, hesitate in the presence of adversity, negotiate at the table of the enemy, ponder at the pool of popularity, wilt in the heat of the battle or meander in the maze of mediocrity.

I won't give up, shut up, let up, or burn up until I've preached up, prayed up, paid up, stored up, worked up and stayed up for the cause of Christ. I am part of the Fellowship of the Unashamed. I walk in good company; I am a disciple of Jesus. I must go until He comes, give until I drop, preach until all know, stay until all go and work until He stops. And when He comes to get His own, He'll have no trouble recognizing me...my colors will be clear!

Amen

POTTER AND CLAY

I believe we all need to pray the following prayer...and mean it:

Lord, I'm clay, made soft by the miracle of Your touch; shape me into whatever, whenever, however, for as long-ever, and for whomever! As clay, I'm open to the shape You will make of me.

If You fashion me into a wedge, I'll gladly hold the door open for Your gospel to go through to all the world. If You press me into a wheel, I'll roll to Your destination; if You mold me into a cup, I'll hold water for one of Your disciples; if You press me into an altar, I'll gladly be knelt upon by any You choose. If You shape me into a scroll, write on me what You will for any to read. If You rub me into a baton, use me to conduct Your symphony.

If You bend me into a flask, I'll hold Your sweet perfume; if You block me into a vase, I'll hold whatever flowers You arrange; if You spin me into a plate, I'll willingly hold food for others; if You pinch me into an arrow, I'll quickly speed to Your target. If You create of me a bush, I'll burn for whatever prophet You choose to watch; if You make me into a tree, I'll shade Your weary pilgrims; if You twist me into a trumpet, I'll gladly be blown for Your praise and glory; if You turn me into a pair of shoes, I'll gladly be walked on to serve others, if

You fashion me into a plaque, I'll gladly be hung on any wall to display Your handiwork.

Lord...You're the potter, I'm the clay...keep me soft, moldable, ready to be shaped into whatever You desire. And Lord, when the molding is done, and my clay is hard, I'll not seek to be something other than what You've made me. Teach me anew that whatever it is, it is an original!!

Prayer for Usefulness

Dear God, I want to be used of You! I've been won to witness, not just watch; saved to serve, not just sit; ransomed to run, not just rot; delivered to demonstrate, not just deliberate. Wash me clean from all the debris and dinginess of drab duty, O God, and get me off the dime of a do-nothing and dreary docket.

Shake from my life all the lethal lethargy that lurks and lingers and lulls me to sleep! Cauterize me from casual living and stinking thinking.

Break my pride, bend my knees, loosen my tongue, open my purse, lift my hands, move my feet. Increase my empathy, strengthen my vision and stir my spirit to aggressive action!

Purge from my life all the dross, all the residue, the redundant, the ridiculous and the repellent, and replace it with resoluteness! Purge me of the putrid, the paltry, and the pitiful and rib me with the steel of courage and commitment that is highly contagious.

In a world of ease and comfort, Lord, thrust me into the fray of battle. Save me from the proneness to sit and watch, from the tendency to let someone else

carry the load, from the inclination to evade and avoid
my part of the battle. Lord, make me useful to You.
Get me off the shelf, under Your power, into the battle.

Amen

So You Want to Be a Disciple

S o you want to be a disciple of Jesus? You want to cast your lot with Him? You want to be identified as one of His? I bid you count the cost, appraise the sacrifice, contemplate long and hard before you leap!

So, you want to be a disciple? Then expect hardship, rejection, discrimination, work, ill-treatment, no-thank-yous, misunderstanding, misinterpretation, misuse and misinformation. Do you want to be a disciple? Get ready for action...for hardship...for tiredness...for deprivation and loneliness.

So you want to be a disciple? Be ready to pay any price, go any distance, penetrate any barrier, climb any mountain, swim any river, scale any height, descend to any depth and work any length as a servant of Jesus Christ. Be prepared to spend and be spent; to go or stay; to walk or lie down; to speak or be silent; to go forward or backward.

So you want to be a disciple? Be ready to walk with Jesus when He walks through fields of unpopularity, streets of hostility, and roads of rejection. Be prepared to follow, even when His steps take you through suffering, persecution, humiliation and yes, maybe even death. Be ready for living or dying; nothing or everything; giving or receiving; coming or going; rest or work; peace or war.

That's the price...and it never goes on sale!

THE AFFIRMATION OF ABANDONMENT

Lord, I've made the plunge. I have become a disciple of Yours. I'm sold out...keep me or send me; fill me or empty me; tear me down or build me up; clothe me or strip me. I've made the choice, stepped over the line, raised my hands in surrender and filed the disclaimer to my life.

You are the King and I'm the subject. You are the Master and I'm the slave. You are the Manager and I'm the body. You are the Drive-train and I'm the wheels. You are the Engine and I'm the propeller.

I'm willing to go, stay, speak, sing, work, walk, talk, pray, serve, live or die...I'm perfectly willing to be possessed by You. Lord, be the Producer and Director of my life. Write my lines, receive the applause, take the bows and get the glory.

Lord, I've "joined up" for action and combat. I'm willing to go the distance, pay the price, suffer the loss, incur the consequences, bear the guff, be a fool and accept the stigma of being different.

I'm a disciple of Yours and here I relinquish all rights, shelve all demands and defer all requests for leaves.

THE SERVANT'S BEATITUDES

B lessed are those who volunteer to work in the kingdom, for they are indeed few.

Blessed are those who work cheerfully, without complaint, for they are a joy to be with.

Blessed are those who stay with their task, for they aren't quitters.

Blessed are those who never complain about their tasks, for they are used of God.

Blessed are the tithers who tithe willingly, for they get it all back anyway.

Blessed are those who don't care who gets the credit for what they do, for their reward is great in heaven.

Blessed is the caller who uses tact and poise, for they won't drive people away.

Blessed are those who work in the nursery, for they will receive a double crown.

Blessed are the faithful who never get recognition, for they will get a great one in heaven.

Blessed are the sponsors of junior high, for they will get a medal for bravery.

Blessed are the optimistic in the faith, for they will win the world.

Blessed are those who share their faith, for they guarantee the future of the church.

Blessed are the greeters at the front door, for they make or break a first time visit.

Blessed are those who stay awake during the preaching, for they shall be edified.

Blessed are the church custodians, for they make God's house beautiful.

Blessed are the senior citizens, for they have stood the test of time.

Blessed are the ushers who serve, for they'll be first to be greeted in heaven.

DENTITY

*Who are you? Oh, you can give
me your name, address, and phone
number, but you still haven't told me who you are.
You might tell me where you work, to whom you're
married, how many children you have, and what
kind of car you drive, but you still haven't told me
who you are. You might tell me your age, your
weight, your height, your hobbies, and your golf
score, but you still haven't divulged your identity.
We're more than our name, our number, and our
niche in life. Our identity is bound up in our
relationship (or lack of relationship) with God.
Many Christians don't even know who they are in
Christ today, thus when problems come and
challenges arrive, they fall to pieces because they
have an identity crisis.*

*We need a fresh new voice telling us that
we're children of God by faith in Jesus Christ,
cleansed and forgiven of all sin, and destined for
heaven. We also need to hear we're not alone, but
have many fellow-travelers with whom to make
this short journey through life.*

A MANDATE TO SATAN

Satan, take note and listen well! Get off my back! You will not conquer me. I'm blood-washed, Spirit-filled, daily delivered, strongly sanctified, Spirit-soaked and Word indwelt. I am linked with sovereign and eternal power and have set my face.

You're a deceiver, but you won't deceive me; you're a liar, but you won't lie to me; you're a killer, but you won't murder me; you're a roaring lion, but I'm not devourable; you're extremely subtle, but I'm on to your ways! You parade as an angel of light, but I walk in a brighter light. Your days of deception are over with me. I won't be deceived, detoured, derailed, distorted, distracted, discouraged or disillusioned by your schemes. Your vile influence won't cross the "No Trespassing" sign on the door of my heart. My life is off-limits to you now. My doors are all closed to you forever! You won't walk in, crawl in, slither in, sneak in, pry in, jump in, swim in, fly in, drive in or barge into my life. I have a permanent guest that now lives inside and He cannot share my temple with you.

You may lure, lie, linger, lurch, laugh, lunge or leap, but you won't come in. Your days are numbered; your kingdom doomed; your designs are dwindling; your evil eroding; your devilishness dissolving; your deceit decaying; your deception diminishing and your death is dying. Your progress is poisoned, your poison is paralyzed and your penetration is profitless! Your ultimate victory has been canceled and soon your show will be over!

You can't trap me with your wares, soil me with your subtlety, or defeat me with your deception. He that is in me is greater than you! Now get off my property, for the day of your final binding is not far away!

A Sense of Direction

I am saved, sanctified, surrendered and sent. I've caught the vision, I'm on the venture, I can see the victory, I can feel the valor, I've become valiant and vocal. The hour is late, the situation desperate, and the need urgent. I must run, not walk; speak now, not later; act, not tarry; preach, not pamper; confront, not coddle; move, not meander; speak, not sputter; proclaim, not procrastinate; share, not shirk; soar, not sit; burn, not smolder.

I cannot wait; I must not linger; I dare not stop; I will not defer; I've set my course. I won't look back, let up, lie down or let loose. The world is lost, and time is now. Man is doomed, sin is rampant, the Lord is ready, the harvest waiting, the gospel powerful, the spirit convicting, the need is great. There is no time for elaborate plans, for casualness, caroling, curtailing, conforming or conferring...no time for detours, coffee breaks, sick leaves or sabbaticals, the curtain is falling, the act is over, the players are leaving, the lights are out, no time-outs left, the band is marching off the field, the clock is stopped, the game is over, we can wait no longer.

I'm headed for a new city and a new home where I'll dwell with a new name in a new age. I know where I've been, I know where I am, and I know where I'm going...the time is now!

God's People

Have you ever heard a description of God's people? They're different. These are God's people; twice born, once committed, marching in step to the music and beat of a distant band. They are invincible, indomitable, indestructible and indelible. They won't be bought, bribed, bent or busted. They are undaunted, undefeated, unconditional and under orders. They're headed for a city whose builder and maker is God. They won't be lured by lewdness, pampered by pleasures, siphoned off by suaveness or drawn away by dreariness. Their gait is set, their goal is clear, their weapons sharpened, their plan is drawn, their vision high, their options few and their victory sure.

These are God's people! They know where they've been, where they are, and where they are going. They get their plan from the Word, their light from the Son, their power from the Spirit...and their direction from God. They won't be diluted by deception, lured by licentiousness, scared by Satan, wearied by woes, derailed by detours or boggled by barriers. They're on their way, marching with heads high, strides long and arms ready for battle.

These are God's people, with determination on their faces, steadfastness in their feet, light in their eyes, and faith in their spirits. They speak another language in which some words are not found. Words like quit, turn back, stop, discouragement, can't and won't. They will win when others lose, conquer when others are subdued, finish when others won't, and praise when others pout. These are God's people!

Do you belong to this army? It is the Fellowship of the Unashamed, the Company of the Committed, the Corps of the Conquerors; they follow one leader, King Jesus!

HEY WORLD, HEAR THIS!

HEY WORLD! I'm a Christian. I'm blood bought, twice born, changed, redeemed, forgiven, filled, sealed, saved and sanctified. Your dirt no longer soils me, your treasures will not spoil me, your values won't control me, your will not standards hold me, nor can your life-style suit me. I cannot be your friend, accommodate your program, approve your music, nor be conciliatory to your position. I cannot date you, condone you, uphold you, defend you, praise you, tolerate you, negotiate with you, or be taught by you. I cannot profit by your means, indulge in your schemes, or share in your dreams. Friendship with you invites enmity with God. I will not be sold to your system, led by your light, taught by your false wisdom, made glad by your wine, feast on your food, be made lovely by your glamour, be made glad by your song, be cheered by your laughter, or be inspired by your verses. I am a Christian...I will not march to your beat, bow at your feet, laugh at your jokes, subscribe to your wisdom, or succumb to your pressure.

Your method is deception, your goal is destruction, your end is decay, your luster is fading, your values decaying, your charm is deceiving, your hope is molding, your returns are dwindling, your disciples are dying and you're passing away.

HEY WORLD! I'm a Christian, I must live IN you, but I'm not OF you. When the shakedown comes, you will crumble but I will abide.

Know Who You Are

I am a Christian! Unworthy, sinful, vile, inherently impure, yet saved and made clean by grace. The blood has been applied, the stain has been removed, the sin is forgiven, the name has been changed and terms have been settled...I'm a child of God forever.

All rights have been relinquished, self-will has been broken, pride has been shattered, coldness has been melted, the gait has been set, the commitment has been made, the purchase completed. I am now the property of Jesus Christ.

I have counted the cost, weighed the consequences, considered the alternatives, anticipated the opposition, calculated the loss, taken up the cross, entered the gate, abandoned the self, made the plunge and I now belong to another. I am cleansed, filled, empowered, graced, warmed, supplied, changed, loved and lifted.

I will not be siphoned away by the subtlety of ease and pleasure, nor lulled to sleep by the deception of apathy, not slowed by sluggishness, not whiled away by whims, not fooled by fads, nor disqualified by disbelief.

I am now a child of God by faith in Jesus Christ, twice born, radically redeemed, compellingly converted, dynamically delivered, soundly sanctified and serenely secure.

I have placed myself totally under the Lordship of Jesus Christ, and I will not be moved!

Plain Ol' Vanilla

Dear God: I may be vanilla, but I'm made of real cream! Though vanilla, today I confess my flavorable position in You. I'm blood-bought, Spirit-filled, 'sin-atized,' daily directed, power possessed, saved forever; a child of the King and an heir coming into an inheritance whose amount is incalculable.

Oh Lord...amidst the sometimes demeaning dreariness of my seemingly dwarfed significance, remind me anew of my infinite worth in You...jog my memory to remember that He who is in me is greater than he that is in the world. Strip me of all that would suggest that I'm valueless, cheap, insignificant and quite dispensable. Reassure me that with You, I count; I matter; I'm important, valuable, essential and have inestimable worth! In a world where everything is measured in size, weight, monetary value, talent, popularity and fame, remind me again that in Your Kingdom, things are measured quite differently.

Show me again that the battle is still not always to the swift and the strong. Deliver me from the deadliness of a do-nothingness attitude because I'm only vanilla. Open the curtain of history and show me again your Hero Hall of Fame, most of whom were vanilla people like me, but charged by Your power.

While I may never stand before thrones, or sing before royalty, or march before dignitaries, or bow to standing ovations, show me again today that I'm vital to Your Kingdom, though vanilla.

And Lord, though vanilla, I'm willing to be topped with your colorful and flavorful toppings that I may attract those You've called me to minister to through a vanilla vessel.

Amen

Prayer of an Average Christian

Dear Lord,
I'm weak, but claim Your power; sinful, but accept Your cleansing; wayward, yet desire Your leading; and dark, but need Your light. Lord, I'm weary, but confess Your strength; lonely, but acknowledge Your presence; in turmoil, but resting in Your peace; impatient, yet trusting in You; impetuous, so I need Your calmness; prone to sin, so I need Your nudging. Lord, I'm often unreliable, so I need Your faithfulness; quick tempered, and thus need Your presence. I believe, Lord, help my unbelief.

I trust, Lord, help my lack of trust. I love You, Lord, help my lovelessness. I'm committed to You, Lord, help my wavering. I'm a disciple, but have feet of clay, so hold me very close, Lord, and keep the light of Your countenance on my face at all times.

Amen.

THE PEOPLE IT WILL TAKE

God needs changed people! He needs a people whose past is forgiven and they know it; people whose present is purposeful and they show it; and people whose future is secured! He needs holy people, people of vision, people of audacity, bold people, brave people; people who dare to dream big dreams and see large visions; people who are willing to pay the price, make the sacrifice, try the difficult, attempt the impossible; people who will sail against the wind, even when sails are battered and vessels are broken.

God needs people whose lives are in drive, not park; people who won't shut up, let up, slow up, dry up, or give up till the task is done! He needs people who won't whine or groan, or make deals, or compromise, or drag their heels. He needs people who will talk Him up and sin down. He needs people who will love the lost, loathe the lurid, like the lovely, lessen the lethargy, liberate the lonely, and live the life.

He needs the prophet to proclaim the Word; the teacher to impart the truth; the counselor with empathetic ears; the servant who never cares who gets the credit. He needs people who won't flinch when the cost is heavy; people who won't retreat when defeat is apparent; people who won't change their colors when the pressure's on; people who won't abandon the sinking ship; and people who refuse to live in the house of mediocrity.

God needs people who are blood-bought, Spirit-filled, power-laden, sin-delivered and Heaven-bound...people who aren't afraid to preach the Bible-true, sin-black, hell-hot, forgiveness-sure and Jesus coming soon!

It was these kinds of people who built arks, stormed cities, marched around Jerichos, crossed Red Seas, shut the mouths of lions and killed giants. It will be these kinds of people God will use to shake the world in the 90's for His cause and Kingdom! Will you be one?

THIS IS WHO WE ARE

We are the Church of the victorious King! We are indomitable! Our message is redemption! Our messengers are God-anointed! Our power supply is nothing less than Heaven! We are the Church, blood bought, boldly built, God's Army, Air Force, Navy and Marines, all wrapped up in one. Our troops are invincible, our Captain is unconquerable, our mission unquenchable, and our target is un-missable!

Our weapons far exceed nuclear weapons and make them look like cap pistols...our weapons are divine, destroying strongholds, penetrating the impenetrable, delivering the lethal blow to the powers and principalities of the world of evil. We are the church, the only army in history that doesn't fight its own battles, for the battle is the Lord's. We are the Church, misunderstood, abused, scarred, bruised, scorned, maligned, avoided, neglected and laughed at, but triumphant, victorious and everlasting.

No kingdom can stop us, no weapons do us in, no detours derail us, no plans destroy us, no set-backs daunt us. We are the Church of the living God, and our cue doesn't come from this world. There is no stopping our aggression, no changing our direction, no cooling our affection, and no changing our confession! We're marching to Zion nonstop and won't be delayed by casual excursions into the tourist traps of this world.

If Jesus is your King, come join us. If not, don't bother, you'll just be dead weight. If you mean business, get on board, if you're ready for hard work, high sacrifice, few compliments, and many challenges, then welcome aboard! We're the Church...the Kingdom that cannot be shaken, we're on our way!!!

WELCOME TO OUR WORLD

Welcome to our world son! You have been nine months forming hands, eyes, legs, hair, and face, but you were planned by God of all eternity. You are a tiny living miracle; the result of love between your mother and me.

You're the one product that is not made on the assembly line. You weren't ordered from a catalog, requisitioned from a computer, designed by a committee, or delivered by mail.

You're not plugged into current, yet you move. You are not attached to a compressor, yet you breathe. You have no sound system, yet you cry. And, you were born hungry with the capacity to eat. Your mother didn't make you, she only contained you. The design for your body and your color coordination is all original. Your model will never be duplicated or copied; you're an original!

Your designer's name is God, and it is He who gives you life, who makes you see, who makes you breathe and enables you to eat. You will grow and develop without the aid of human technology or scientific expertise.

You are potentially a father, a grandfather, and a great-grandfather. Your stay here is indefinite. One thing is for sure...you have arrived with a round-trip-ticket, and someday you will return to the God who sent you. But, for today, welcome to our world!

Today I dedicate you and set you apart to serve the living God all the days of your earthly life. I commit myself to love you, provide for you, and be there when you hurt. I am your father, and you have been loaned to me by God to care for and return someday. I promise you I will do my very best.

Love,

Your Dad

You Count

No one needs to be a nobody! In an age of computers and cartridges, account numbers and technology, man has fallen prey to the disease of insignificance. It's demeaning, to say in the least, to arrive at the office and discover that you and five others have been replaced by a computer. The Bible has a lot to say about man.

Though he is a fallen creature, he is unique and deeply significant. He is precious to God. I think as never before, man needs to hear that he counts, he matters, he's significant, important, and in fact quite indispensable. In an age of mass production, conglomerates, and where everything is identified by a number, area code, zip code, social security number, bank number, house number and lot number, man needs to know that he's more than a mere number.

Peter in his Epistle says, "You are a chosen race, a royal priesthood, a holy nation, God's own people." The Psalmist said, "What is man that thou are mindful of him ... for thou hast made him a little less than God." Friend, we are God's highest form of creation. We were created for fellowship with the eternal God.

Heaven hasn't been prepared for a number, Christ didn't die for a statistic, the Kingdom of God isn't inhabited by lot numbers, you are the one who counts and matters to God. So, if you've felt left out lately, like you don't count, you don't matter, I have good news for you. You do. So live as if you are the one for whom Christ died and rose again because you are.

LORDSHIP

The Greek word for "Lord" in the Bible is the same word we use for a master, like in a slave-master setting. You cannot receive Jesus as Savior only. His Lordship is bound up in His Saviorhood and visa-versa. We cannot "make" Him Lord. He already is. What we can do is personally acknowledge Him as Lord. But in doing so, we establish a unique relationship where we literally become His servant or slave. A slave has three basic characteristics; he doesn't belong to himself, but to another. Secondly, he has been purchased with a price. In our case, that price was the blood of Christ. And thirdly, he's in that relationship on a permanent basis, or until he's "sold" to another master. Since we're eternally His, our relationship is permanent. Jesus is an unusual Master because He alone sets us free from sin, death, and ourselves. What an honor to be His slave as opposed to being a slave of the devil. Someone has well said that before we were saved, we were slaves of the devil. After we're saved, we're still slaves, but the difference is we've changed masters.

ॐ   ॐ   ॐ

Branded for Christ

Lord, brand me with Your kind of Christianity...the kind that sees large visions...that dreams great dreams...that doesn't tolerate the insipid, the bland and the average!

Burn within my life an uncontrollable, compulsive hunger and thirst for You...a ravenous compassion and concern for the lost...a militant intolerance of mediocrity, getting by, and harmless 'temperance' when it comes to doing Your will!

Mark me indelibly with Your branding iron so there will be no question as to whose I am...renovate my tongue to speak only Your praise...redirect my feet to follow You and You alone...re-aim my sight to look at my world through Your eyes and Yours alone.

Press upon me Lord, that brand of Christianity that is urgent and has unction, one that goes for broke, walks by faith, gives lavishly, serves gladly and prays ferociously!

Amen

CONFESSION OF A SLAVE

I t was a great day in America when Abraham Lincoln signed the Emancipation Proclamation, thus freeing all slaves, and bringing to an end an ungodly system of inequity. When that Proclamation was signed, slaves would never again be bought and sold on the auction block like cattle. Even the talk of a slavery system today brings chills to the twentieth century culture.

Another Emancipation Proclamation was signed over 2,000 years ago when Jesus died and shed His blood on the cross. That death freed man from the bondage and tyranny of sin. That's why Paul wrote that sin will have no dominion of you (Romans 6:14). But there is an irony in our emancipation. Before a person is saved, he is a slave to a cruel taskmaster, sin. After he is saved, he doesn't lose his status as a slave, but simply changes masters.

Six times the writers of the epistles referred to themselves as "slaves of Jesus Christ." A slave is one who has been bought with a price, and is the sole property of a particular owner. A missing dimension in contemporary Christianity that boasts of soft pews, soft lights, short sermons, relatively little involvement, is the fact that if we are saved, we are also slaves of Jesus Christ. The truth is, however, we don't often act like slaves. We do what we want to do, go where we want to go, spend what we want to spend and be what we want to be, often with little or no regard to the wishes of our new owner. I think we need to reinstate the following confession of a slave of Jesus Christ:

Master, this is Your slave, bought with a price, ransomed from sin and totally Yours. I'm sold out, surrendered; I've stepped over the line, made the decision and settled the issue. I've forfeited my right to ever say no to anything You ask...Lord; I'm Yours and Yours alone, nothing held back! You graciously bought me off the slave block. The title of my ownership has been changed. I once belonged to another master who used and abused me, but your death on the cross released his grip. I'm now under Your domain, Your control, at Your disposal, under Your authority and Your direction.

Because I am Yours, empty me or fill me, send me or keep me here, humble me or exalt me, reduce me or enlarge me, multiply me or subtract me, push me or pull me, raise me or lower me, run me or walk me, put me in forward or reverse, strip me or decorate me, bind me or loosen me, display me or conceal me, mobilize me or make me stationary. I'm Yours, Lord, all Yours.

CONFESSION OF A TRUE CHRISTIAN

I've seen the light, counted the cost, made the choice, settled the question, resolved the conflict, stepped over the line, forsaken the self. I've rendered the decision, and I've become the follower of Jesus Christ. I've renounced all ownership, claimed all promises, met all conditions. I have opted for life, not death; innocence, not guilt; light, not darkness; and heaven not hell. I've signed the covenant, agreed to the terms, read the fine print, met the Author, joined the ranks and burned the bridges.

The choice is made, the direction is determined, the combat entered, the weapons readied, the ear is tuned and eye is set. I've become a soldier of the cross and my term is life. I'm ready to go or stay, wait or move, walk or run, laugh or cry, lift or be lifted, be first or last, now or later, be whatever, whenever for however long. I'm a Christian, and I'm not my own anymore. I've sold out, turned out, been bought out, and will burn out if need be. I will go, work, pray, sit, stand, crawl, limp, trot, run, speak or wait. I'm now at His disposal. I won't retreat, renege, return or reconsider. I've entered the race and my future belongs to Christ.

STATE OF THE ART

I t dawned on me recently that Jesus is "State of the Art." He is the utopia, the highest, the best, none other can compare. He is the way, the truth, the life. He is the King of Kings, the Lord of Lords, the God of all Gods, the first and the last, the beginning and the end. He is the Rose of Sharon, the Bright and Morning Star, The Lily of the Valley. When you have Jesus, you may not have much of this world's goods, but you have everything. When you don't have Jesus, you may be overflowing with the things of this world, but you have nothing.

In Him is life, deliverance, power, joy, fulfillment, forgiveness, hope, and meaning. Without Him, we simply die in our sins. If we miss Jesus we've missed it all. He is exalted above all, and is the one who will return personally to this earth to gather His own someday.

Some who have never traveled will take that trip because they now know Him. Some who have traveled extensively all over the world will miss that trip because they don't know Him. If you don't know Him personally, let me ask you to invite Him into your life, right now, before it's too late. He truly is "State of the Art" and He makes us the same when we belong to Him.

ARRIAGE

Someone said that marriage is three weeks of curiosity, three months of love, and thirty years of tolerance! Someone else said that marriage is a proposition ending in a sentence! Let's hope not. Many humorous things are said about the institution of marriage, but the truth is, of all human relationships, it's got to be highest, the sweetest, the most sacred, and the most fulfilling. No wonder...God is the author of marriage. He thought it up, designed it, then created it. Marriage is leaving, cleaving, conceiving, and believing in each other. It's the only math where one plus one equals one! Marriage can never be a 50-50 proposition. It's always 100-100. Both spouses must give 100 percent to make it work smoothly. Ninety percent of the success of any marriage depends on attitude. If you will to serve, honor, and love your spouse, your marriage will be an astounding success. If you sit back and only wait for your spouse to do that, it will get out of kilter fast! Remember, what God has joined together, let not man put asunder. It's for real, for life, and it's up to you to keep the termites out and the preservatives in!

A Parent's Prayer

O h, heavenly Father, make me a better parent. Teach me to understand my children, to listen patiently to what they have to say, and to answer all their questions kindly. Keep me from interrupting them or contradicting them. Make me as courteous to them as I would have them be to me. Forbid that I should ever laugh at their mistakes, or resort to shame or ridicule when they displease me.

May I never punish them for my own selfish satisfaction or to show my power. Let me not tempt my child to lie or steal. And guide me hour by hour that I may demonstrate by all I say and do that honesty produces happiness.

Reduce, I pray, the meanness in me. And, when I am out of sorts, help me, Oh Lord, to hold my tongue. May I ever be mindful that my children are children and I should not expect of them the judgment of adults. Let me not rob them of the opportunity to wait on themselves and to make decisions.

Bless me with the bigness to grant them all their reasonable requests and the courage to deny them privileges I know will do them harm. Make me fair and just and kind. And fit me, Oh Lord, to be loved and respected and imitated by my children.

Amen

A Husband's Prayer

O Lord, I lift to you the most prized possession of my life...my dear wife. Forgive me, Lord, for assuming too much...forgive the foolishness of taking her for granted. Redeem me, O Lord, from the sin of insensitivity and indifference. Deliver me, O Lord, from failure to cherish her as the apple of my eye, the most prized possession of my life...from listening but not hearing, from being miles away while I'm with her at home. Purge me, O Lord, from the busy-ness that consumes my attention, leaving none for her. Cleanse me, O God, of the cutting and catty remarks I've made to her, the careless and often delayed response when she asks me a question...or makes a simple statement to me.

Lord, fill my mouth with praise for her instead of complaints, with positive words instead of negative words; with stroking words instead of grating words; with smooth words instead of harsh words. Lord, this is my wife...may there be no time in her life that her spirit is injured by what I say...or don't say, or say wrongly, or say too loudly. Show me how to cherish her, lift her, exalt her, placing her at the correct spot on my scale of values. Show me how to feed and nurture her, build her up, alleviate her fears, banish her doubts, scatter her gloom, wipe her tears and bandage up her hurts in such a way that she knows, beyond a shadow of a doubt, that I love her above anyone else on this earth. Teach me how to put her first, raise her high, protect her from harm, and be a strong tower in her time of storm.

Lord, this is my wife you've created for me...may I never use her, but love her; may I never thwart her but encourage her; may I never put her down, but lift her; may I never smother her, but free her; may I never embarrass her, but always make her feel she is an integral part of me. Give her strength for harder days, so when life has had its day, she'll look back and with gratitude say...HE CARED...HE WAITED...HE GAVE HIS BEST FOR ME.

A Stander's Affirmation

I am standing for the healing of my marriage! I will not give up, give in, give out or give over, until that healing takes place. I made a vow, I said the words, I gave the pledge, I gave a ring, I took a ring, I gave myself, I trusted God, and said the words, and meant the words...in sickness and in health, in sorrow and in joy, for better or for worse, for richer or for poorer, in good times and in bad. So, I am standing now, and will not sit down, let down, slow down, calm down, fall down, or be down until the breakdown is torn down!

I refuse to put my eyes on outward circumstances, or listen to prophets of doom, or buy into what is trendy, worldly, popular, convenient, easy, quick, thrifty or advantageous...nor will I settle for a cheap imitation of God's real thing, nor will I seek to lower God's standard, twist God's will, rewrite God's Word, violate God's covenant, or accept what God hates, namely divorce!

In a world of filth, I will stay pure; surrounded by lies I will speak the truth; where hopelessness abounds I will hope in God; where revenge is easier I will bless instead of curse; and where the odds are stacked against me, I will trust in God's faithfulness.

I am a stander, and I will not compromise, quarrel or quit. I have made the choice, set my face, entered the race, believed the Word, and trusted God for all the outcome.

I will allow neither the reaction of my spouse, nor the urging of my friends, nor the advice of my loved ones, nor economic hardship, nor the prompting of the devil to make me let up, slow up, or give up until my marriage is healed!

EXTERMINATE YOUR MARRIAGE

I f you pulled back the curtains and opened the cabinets of many marriages, you would find a multitude of insect pests eating away at that marriage. Here are some pests that must be exterminated before it's too late...

THE ANT OF ABSENCE: Husbands are notorious for "vacating the premises." The "never home" syndrome usually ends in divorce by desertion.

THE ROACH OF RESENTMENT: Harboring ill-will against your spouse can build and build until an explosion happens. Whatever it is...get it out in the open and take care of it.

THE BEE OF BERATING: Constant berating of one another wears thin! Couples who let this pest of criticism run rampant in their marriage see the attorney sooner than expected. This bee's sting has poison in it and has a way of destroying whatever it stings.

THE MOSQUITO OF MOODINESS: This pest really takes its toll. Moody partners suck the very life-blood out of a marriage. This pest must go at all cost.

THE FLY OF FLIRTATION: This pest causes spouses to "buzz" from one person to another flirting and asking for trouble. This fly must be swatted early on in any marriage.

THE GNAT OF NARCISSISM: A narcissistic person is a selfish person...everything is for self; they must have their own way. This pest, if left to itself, will "carry away" its victims into a world of self-centeredness.

THE TERMITE OF TOUGHNESS: A "be tough" position in marriage is like a termite that quietly eats away the foundation of a house. Unseen and unheard, this creature slowly eats away in an area few can see. A "tough" and unyielding attitude destroys marriages like termites destroy houses.

THE BEETLE OF BOOZE: This insect has destroyed more homes than one can count. Where one or both partners are drinkers, they soon reap what they have sown. This pest is best controlled by not allowing him in to start with!

THE MOTH OF MURMURING: A murmuring spirit in marriage eats away at its fiber. A spirit of complaining, griping and whining will destroy a marriage like a moth destroys a fur coat.

These "pests" have no place in your marriage. The greatest and most effective destroyer of these pests is the Word of God restored in your marriage. Try it!

Marriage Love or Phoney Love

There is a difference in 'marriage' love and 'phony' love. Marriage love is concerned with giving, phony love tries to get. Marriage love forfeits rights, phony love forfeits nothing. Marriage love always builds up, phony love tears down. Marriage love serves the other, phony love demands service. Marriage love says I'm sorry, phony love says you ought to be.

Marriage love makes requests, phony love makes demands. Marriage love makes provisions, phony love makes excuses. Marriage love will sacrifice, phony love will not be inconvenienced. Marriage love goes the second mile, phony love never completes the first mile. Marriage love remembers, phony love forgets. Marriage love minimizes the faults of the other, phony love magnifies the faults of his/her mate.

Marriage love apologizes, phony love justifies. Marriage love learns to wait, phony love goes ahead. Marriage love praises, but phony love condemns. Marriage love gives compliments, phony love finds fault. Marriage love negotiates, phony love dictates. Marriage love anticipates, phony love agitates.

Marriage love overlooks, phony love detects.

Marriage love listens long, phony love speaks too long. Marriage love will try again and again, phony love gives up after the first try.

A PRAYER FOR MY WIFE

L ord, this is my wife. I've committed my earthly life to her. Help me love her like You love the church: sacrificially, long, and unwavering. Let there be no moment in her life she doubts my fidelity, my care, and my concern. As her husband, O God, burn away my blemishes with the skill of the surgeon You are. O Lord, cut away from my life imperfections, defects, the undesirable, and the unacceptable. Teach me, Lord, that my provision for her is more than food, clothing and shelter; there is also assurance, affection, adulation and attention. Strip me, Lord, from poisonous pride, insidious insensitivity, constant complaining, incessant inattention, and devilish downgrading.

O Lord, this is my wife, show me how to nourish her with the Bread of Life; enable me to cherish her with singleness of heart. May I never take her for granted or treat her like a wash-woman or the cook, or the servant of the house. Dear God, enable me, as a husband, to focus on my responsibilities, not my rights; on my duties, not demands; on my love for her, not her favors for me.

O Lord, this is my wife...let not one day pass

when she doesn't feel she is the most important person in my life. Lord, let not the years dim the twinkle in my eye, nor fade the love in my heart, nor place a gap between us. Rather, let the passage of time serve like a magnet that pulls us closer together, so the last of our years will be more romantic than the first. And, if by Your providence I am called home before her, may her remarriage be proof that I so fulfilled her life she would never live without a husband.

Amen

PRAYER OF THE BRIDEGROOM

My beloved, today is the day of days. Our hopes, our dreams, our longings, our yearnings find fulfillment...Today we walk an aisle...Today when we say 'I love you' it's set in concrete...Today, in the sight of God, we make a vow to one another...Today we kneel together in the awesome presence of God...Today we take the final step...Today that mystical union becomes a reality...Today we become one...Today I enter you, and you enter me, and we, together, enter God in a special way.

Today part of my individuality goes, and so does yours...Today a ring will symbolically announce to all present that we are serious about our commitment... Today you become my wife...Today God grants me the key to the golden and precious intimacies of your life. For months I've stood on the porch, today I come in and sup with you and you with me.

Today God joins us together with something stronger than super glue...Today our love, our strengths, our weaknesses, our highest ambitions will merge into one flesh...Today we settle our relationship to one another until death calls one of us home...Today the dye is cast, the partner chosen, the decision made...Today we become one!

Above and beyond the glow of the candles, the glitter of the decorations, and the fragrance of the flowers, I'll see you, alive, bright, pure, smiling, waiting, longing to be one with me. And, when the last note on the organ has finished, the last candle has gone out, the last piece of cake has been eaten, the last glass of punch has been emptied, we will walk into the future brave, happy, excited, jubilant, but most importantly, as one.

Your Bridegroom

TEN COMMANDMENTS FOR MARITAL BLISS

Thou shalt have no other task before thee than fulfilling the needs of thy spouse.

Thou shalt never, shalt never raise thy voice except in case of fire.

Thou shalt always find reason to compliment and praise thy spouse.

Thou shalt remember who thy spouse must live with in order to be more understanding.

Thou shalt focus on thy responsibility to thy spouse, not theirs to you.

Thou shalt remember thy spouse's birthday in a before the last minute.

Thou shalt always include thy spouse in all thy plans.

Thou shalt schedule special times to be alone with thy spouse in order that closeness will never be destroyed.

Thou shalt go out of thy way to let thy spouse know where they come in your scale of priorities.

Your Daughter's Wedding Day

My little girl, today is your wedding day, the day I always hoped wouldn't come...it's here! Gone are the days of a soft little baby, the toothless grins that later burst into full-fledged smiles. Gone are the days of your first little dress with lace and small buttons...gone are the days when we grabbed the camera to capture your first attempt at crawling. Gone are the sleepless nights because you were cutting your first little tooth.

Gone are the days when we burst with pride as you took three full steps across the kitchen for the first time. Today you will take more first time steps; this time, down a long aisle with me! Gone are the days of suckers in your hands and mouth...and on the wall, and in your hair (and ours).

Gone are the days of color books, balloons at the circus, barrettes, broken dolls, and tea sets...gone are the days of soiled little dresses, skinned knees that received our kisses a thousand times...today you stand tall with no blemishes, in another dress, with other lace, for another reason. Who are you, daughter, so tall, beautiful, smart, and grown? Are you the same little girl who picked me a bouquet at three?...Today you'll hold another bouquet for another man more important now than I — your groom! Are you the little five-year-old girl who talked like a chatterbox about the butterflies, the trick or treat, the clowns and the birthday parties? Today you'll talk again, but this time it will be vows spoken for life to the one you've chosen to marry. Who are you, little girl...are you the same daughter who made a long trip two doors down on your tricycle?

Today you'll make a longer trip halfway across the world with the man you'll marry. Today is your wedding day. No more phones ringing a dozen times a day for you, no more laughter from you at our table, no more endless lines of friends streaming through our house, no more 'please, daddy, please, just this once' rhetoric from your mouth. Today, you change your name, your address, your loyalty, your allegiance and though you'll still be our daughter, it won't be the same, nor should it! Today, our days of molding and shaping are over for you. Today you'll belong to another, and we'll love him too. Today, we'll watch, we'll smile, we'll condone, we'll bless, we'll confirm and we'll rejoice, but we will also weep because it came so soon. Thank you Lord, for the years, for the joy, for the daughter. It's time for the wedding to begin. We love you!

 **ERSONAL**

*You are what you think! You are
what you dream! You are what you
eat! You are a replica of your friends! These and
other pithy sayings may be tried and true, but the
fact is that we are who we are. Sometimes it's
good just to sit and think about nostalgic
things...your first grade teacher, your earliest
memories of your grandmother, your grade school
principal, your first date, getting your driver's
license, your wedding day. It's O.K. to be
nostalgic and think sometimes about your own
personal life, where you've been, where you are,
where you're going...and to remind yourself that
though you're probably not famous, and your
name isn't a household word, you're vitally
important to God.*

A Single's Prayer

Lord, I'm single...I cook my own meals, darn my own socks, change my own oil, drive my own car, clean my own house, play my own stereo, watch my TV all alone, tuck myself into bed, get myself up, and listen to the morning news alone! I do many things, in fact, alone. I live alone, eat alone, sleep alone, drive alone, sit alone, dress alone, plan alone, walk alone, and pay bills alone. I leave an empty house in the morning alone, and return to an empty house alone after work at night. I know the noise of silence, the pain of loneliness, the struggle of relationships and the dragging of weekends.

Lord, I'm single, but I do not ask for pity, just understanding; I don't crave special attention, just a sense of value in your eyes and the eyes of my peers. Grant me the conviction to stay clean, the patience to wait, the wisdom to learn and the desire to serve. Lord, I do not seek marriage, nor do I run from it, bring it if You will, when You will, how You will, and with whom You will. In a couple's world, O Lord, let me have a place to stand, to count, to be, to serve, to contribute, to love and to matter. Lord, You were single on this earth, so I know You understand exactly how I feel...let me follow in Your steps.

Amen

END OF MY ROPE

Lord, it's happened. I'm there...at the end of my rope...barely clinging...but it's slipping from my hands...the pressures have been too much...the trials too great...the night too black...the challenge too large, the weight too heavy.

This is it, Lord, there's no more holding on; I'm out of rope. But, wait...what's that you said? O Lord, did I hear you right? Did you hear me right? Are you serious, Lord? Do you mean what you just said, Lord? Did you really say 'let go' after I managed to hold on all this time?

Let go, Lord? You say it so confidently, like you already know how far I will drop...what's that Lord? You say 'trust me'? But, Lord, you don't know how long I've held on with my own strength. I mean, up to this point I've done pretty well. Now you say 'trust me' and 'let go'.

O.K., God, you asked for it. Get ready - here I go. I'm letting go right now. I did it, Lord. I did it, I mean YOU did it! I let go and You held me. I didn't plummet to the bottom. You held me Lord, You held me.

What's that Lord? Yes, I know you said you would, but then I guess, well, I guess I just didn't believe You, but now I do. Thank You Lord for being there when I came to the end of my rope.

HOMESICK

O Lord, I want to come home...the journey has been so long, so tiring...so exhausting...there have been so many intermittent stops...I want to come home! With wrinkled face...shaking hands...dimmed vision...fading hearing...long days...longer nights...I want to come home. My battles are all fought...my children all raised...my work all done...my mark has been made... my dues are all paid...my dreams all fulfilled...my healthy days gone. I want to come home...I just want to come home.

My retirement is all done...my vacations all used...my adventures all over...trials all endured... I'm ready to come home. O Lord, I'm due for a change of scenery...a change of body...I want to come home.

This earth holds no more frontiers for me now...no more goals...no more horizons...no more battles...no more work...no more play...no more fun...no more rest...no more miles...no more banquets...no more shows...no more breaks...no more holidays...I want to come home, I just want to come home.

My years of life dragged by ever so slowly at first, then rapidly, now ever so slowly again. One day is like a month and one month is like an eternity...Lord, I'm ready...I want to come home.

Lord...I'm almost there...even with dimmed vision,

I can see the glitter of the golden streets...even with gnarled hands, I can almost feel the gates of pearl...even with little hearing, I can hear the trumpets...I'm almost there, Lord, just a little farther, just a little farther. Lord, this house I live in called my body has a ceiling that's turned completely gray...it has walls that are collapsing...doors that creak...shutters that need paint...a yard that needs weeding...and windows overlaid with the dinginess of time.

Lord it's time...I'm ready...don't delay...I'm done with this old residence...the tent has fulfilled its purpose. I've finished the race...I've kept the faith...I'm ready to come home. What's that I hear, Lord? Lord, it is! It's the sound of hoof beats and rolling wheels of the chariot...O thank God the chariot's coming...I can see it now. I'm ready Lord, I'm ready...the homesickness is finally over!

Amen

I AM THE SPIRIT OF DEPRESSION

I am the spirit of depression! I dwell only in people who have their gate open for me to walk into their lives. I dwell in all kinds of people...successful people, failures, wealthy people.

People who are going through some hard knocks...people who have lost their jobs, have broken marriages, their car won't run, the rent is due, and they're out of money. But, I also manage to walk through left-open gates of people who are read up and even prayed up.

When allowed to stay by the persons I indwell, I am able to spread doom and gloom in their life, extract the joy from their walk, bring great pessimism, and create a cynical attitude...I am able to produce sluggishness, tiredness, sleeplessness, loss of appetite and of course devastation to the spiritual life of the person. I am, in fact, one of Satan's most effective strategies to neutralize true believers and render them ineffective for long periods at a time.

I am the spirit of depression! There is no life I won't enter, given the invitation of the open gate. The only people I can't touch are those believers whose commitment to Jesus Christ is the highest thing in their life...people who spend daily time in prayer and the Word...people who never miss church and who are involved in ministering to others. Those folks are off limits to me...there is nothing I can do to get to them, but I won't stop trying. Meanwhile, I continue to indwell those with the open gate. I AM THE SPIRIT OF DEPRESSION! I will enter anyone, anytime, anyway when the gate of their life is unguarded. I am the spirit of depression.

JUST FOR TODAY

Just for today - I will try to live through this day only, and not tackle my whole life's problems at once. I can do something for twelve hours that would appall me if I felt I had to keep it up for a lifetime.

Just for today - I will be happy. This assumes to be true what Abraham Lincoln said, "Most folks are as happy as they make up their minds to be."

Just for today - I will adjust myself to what is, and not try to adjust everything to my own desires; I will take my 'life' as it comes and fit myself to it.

Just for today - I will try to strengthen my mind; I will study, I will learn something useful, I will not be a mental loafer, I will read something that requires effort, thought and concentration.

Just for today - I will exercise my soul in three ways: I will do somebody a good turn, and not get found out; if somebody knows, it will not count. I will do at least two things I don't want to do - just for exercise. I will not show anyone that my feelings are hurt; they may be hurt, but today I will keep it to myself.

Just for today - I will be agreeable. I will look as well as I can, dress becomingly, talk low, act courteously, criticize not one bit, not find fault with anything, and not try to improve or regulate anybody except myself.

Just for today - I will have a plan. I may not follow it exactly, but I will have one. I will save myself from two pests; hurry and indecision.

Just for today - I will have a quiet half hour all by myself and relax. During this half hour I will try to get a better perspective of my life.

Just for today - I will be unafraid. I will enjoy that which is beautiful, and will believe that as I give to the world, so the world will give to me.

THE LAST DAY OF MY LIFE

If today was the last day of my life, surely I would make sure that I was going to heaven. Surely I would settle all unsettled accounts. I would ask forgiveness of all I have offended. I would make sure my family knew I loved them. I would confess to God all known sin in my life and seek His face as never before.

If today was the last day of my life I would surely right all wrongs, straighten out all differences, and curtail all unnecessary activities. I would cancel all my business appointments, my luncheon engagements, my job interview, and my evening at the ball game.

If today was the last day of my life, I would speak to somebody about their soul's salvation; I would make sure my giving was up to God's holy standard; I would make sure I was prayed up, read up, served up, and worked up. If today was the last day of my life, I think I would take a little time to prepare for the longest journey I will ever make.

Well...what would you do if you knew today was the last day of your life? Wouldn't it be something if we were all living the kind of lives God wants us to live, so that upon knowing this was the last day of our life, we would do nothing differently!

TODAY

TODAY I will get a word from God in His book the Bible.

TODAY I will pray; it's God's telecommunication system!

TODAY I will laugh; it will ease the tension of my world.

TODAY I will compliment someone; it may save them from despair.

TODAY I will behold some beauty of God's creation; it's the prelude of praise.

TODAY I will secretly do something for someone else and they'll never know who did it.

TODAY I will let someone else in front of me, so my humility will grow.

TODAY I will touch some life that is hurting, and brighten their world.

TODAY I will at least once return good for evil, and help mold a life.

TODAY I will encourage one person who is down; it may salvage him for all time.

TODAY I will meditate at least once on a great victory; it's music for my soul!

TODAY I will give something to someone, somewhere and make a difference in their life.

Have you ever stopped to think that yesterday is gone forever, you can't call it back, you can't relive it; redo it, or reshape it. Tomorrow is uncertain, and does not even belong to us because it isn't here. We only have today. Whatever we will do in life must be done now, today!

PRAYER

Prayer is to the soul what breathing is to the body. As breathing is necessary for the perpetuity of life, so prayer is necessary for the health of the soul. There are all kinds of praying; regular praying, desperate praying, long praying, short praying, effective praying, and dry praying. But all prayer has one common denominator; it's communion with God, fellowship with God, intercession to God, listening to God. It's true, Satan trembles when he sees the weakest Christian on his knees. Prayer is a mighty force that can move mountains and change us. God is delighted when we pray. God acts when we pray. Someone said, "When I work, I work, but when I pray, God works!" How true that is. We're commanded in scripture to pray without ceasing, to ask, seek, knock, to pray in the Spirit at all times with all prayer and supplication. Hopefully the following will motivate you to pray more.

DEDICATION

Dedication...is more than trying hard...more than getting around to it. It is enduring any inconvenience...in the midst of all kinds of detours, because Jesus comes first. Dedication surges on despite the bad weather, the nasty remarks, the detours, the roadblocks, and the delays. Dedication never flinches at insurmountable obstacles, never cringes at inevitable barricades, never whines at inflated costs, never is intimidated at subtle threats, and is never ready to call it quits. Dedication pays the price, goes the gamut, bites the bullet, plows the ground, flexes the needed muscle and spends itself. Dedication has never heard of words like "quit," "wait," "retreat," "sight," "mediocre," "postpone," and "can't."

Dedication goes to any length, makes any sacrifice, takes any chance, goes to any trouble, spends any amount, climbs any mountain, swims any ocean, assumes any obligation, works out any amount of hours, and does anything to achieve its goal!

Dedication...never gives up, lets up, shuts up, folds up or burns up until the task is finished. Dedication suffers whatever pain, endures whatever strain, forfeits whatever gain, and accepts whatever rain until the finish line is reached. Dedication is an attitude, not a platitude, a way of life, not a commodity. It is a do-or-die, go-for-broke, all-the-way route. Dedication can't be "bought off," dissuaded, cooled off, slowed down, redefined, or put on hold. Dedication is being invincible. It "keeps on going" when all the rest say "throw in the towel." It is nothing less than what Jesus calls for in the life of any would-be disciple.

In fact, Jesus said, "Not everyone who says Lord, Lord, will enter the kingdom of heaven, but he who does the will of my Father who is in heaven." Are you DEDICATED?

MOUNTAIN TO BE MOVED

D o you have a mountain in your life that needs to be moved? Jesus once said: "Truly I say to you, whoever says to this mountain, be taken up and cast into the sea, and does not doubt in his heart, but believes that what he says will come to pass, it will be done for him."

Have you ever pondered that promise? Every life has its mountains. There are mountains of fear, mountains of doubt, mountains of sorrow, mountains of despair, mountains of guilt, mountains of disappointment, mountains of anger, mountains of bitterness, mountains of worry and mountains of sin. What is your mountain today? If it doesn't belong there and you don't want it there, you don't have to call the mountain movers. Jesus said, you are to speak to that mountain with authority and with faith. Notice, he said we are to speak to the mountain directly, and say to it, "Be moved!" Then he said, it will come about when we believe what we have commanded is being done!! When the Bible says that we were created to replenish the earth and subdue it, I believe God was telling us that we have the potential for changing circumstances by his power. The problem is we haven't drawn from that reservoir of power enough.

I would challenge you today, wherever you are, whoever you are, whatever your mountain may be, to address it right now. Speak to that unwanted mountain with the authority of the Lord. Believe that God can and will take it away, then behave accordingly. God has called *us* to be the mountain movers.

Prayer for the President

O God, I pray for Mr. President. Grant him wisdom to make decisions, stamina to survive the pressure, hope to endure the bleakness. With so many voices shouting, Lord, let him hear the still small voice.

With so much advice given him, Lord, let him continue to ask "Is there any word from the Lord?" May he never be wearied by controversies, bought by compromises, confused by chaos or swayed by threats. Let him never confuse wisdom with knowledge, office with ego, position with power, or conviction with convenience.

Let him hold in each hand, O God, the twin powers of the Word of God and the conviction of man. May he never fall into the trap of being a man-pleaser, a tyrant, a coward or a procrastinator. And Lord, when the heat is on, the pressure high, the moment critical, and the hour desperate; may he never flinch, run away, hide, do the politically expedient thing, or bail out.

May he never abandon ship. May he never pacify to stay popular, cajole to stay credible, compromise to stay acceptable, or dilute principle to stay powerful. Above all, O God, amidst the noise and confusion of the rabble, give him vision for a better America and keep his hope fixed on you.

In Jesus Name,

Amen

# RETURN OF CHRIST

Everyone is so busy, they're honking at their own taillights. Very few are even thinking that Christ may return visibly to this earth TODAY. It's a forgotten doctrine, yet the Bible talks about it being our "blessed hope." It will come at an hour we do not expect. The Bible says Jesus will come like a thief in the night. No one ever expects a thief to come, and they usually come at an hour that no one could guess. Though He's coming, we're not just to sit idle until He gets here. We're to "occupy" until He comes, meaning take our place of responsibility...witnessing to as many people as possible before He comes, because after the rapture of the church, it will be too late. The season of soul winning will be over. Will you be at your post of duty between now and then? When He comes, will He find the church on a coffee break, in a committee meeting, or at play? Hopefully He will find us busy with the business of the King!

HERE COMES THE GROOM

She will be battle-scarred and pure! Her members will have faced the battle, made the sacrifice, paid the price, suffered the loss, persevered and emerged triumphant. The Bride will be a stately lady, uncompromising, undiluted, unapologetic, unadulterated, unpopular, and unadorned. She will have stood her ground, passed the test, survived the scrape, endured the flack, followed the Word and have been obedient. She will be ready when the Groom appears...whether in China, Africa, Indonesia, Paraguay, Egypt or Seattle...she will be ready in the morning, at noon or in the evening...she will be ready, regardless. She will be devoid of the phony, the half-hearted, the shirker, the miser, the griper, the compromiser, the complainer, the sight-walker, the spectator, the quitter, the deceiver and the appeaser. She'll be ready and waiting...God's people...the humble, the consistent, the workers, the givers, the go-ers, the prayer-ers, the stay-ers, the say-ers, the faith-walkers. These are the re-born, the regenerate, the revived, the restored, the resurrected, the repentant, the re-dedicated and the redeemed. What a wedding day! What a wedding party! What a reception!

THE EIGHTH LETTER TO THE CHURCH

O waiting Church, get your house in order! I'm on My way...your days on earth are few and numbered... the time is now short! Before I come, dear Church, shore up your shoddiness, peel off your pious platitudes, scrape away the barnacles of your indulgence and indifference...sweep up the dirt and debris you've allowed to gather...unfurl all your flags, pull out all the stops, man your stations, return to your priority...drain out your drudgery, your drowsiness and your dreariness. Sharpen your swords, load your guns, take your positions, aim well, attack your enemy with fierceness and abandon, this is your one last shot.

O Church, your time is about up! You need to strip off your attitude of casualness and 'business as usual' - take your inventory, balance your books. The eleventh hour is only days away!

Redeem yourself, O Church, from insipidness, paltry plans, tardiness, laziness, leniency and lewdness. This is not the time to comfort the disturbed, but to disturb the comfortable; this is not the time to walk, but to run; not a time to sit, but surge. O Church, call sin black, hell hot, the Bible sure, and Jesus coming soon. Cancel all leaves, put nothing on hold, take no time-outs, have done with all coffee breaks...put all the saints on permanent standby.

Have done with dwarfed plans, petty projects and all that is extracurricular. Cease your meaningless meandering, your half-hearted hesitations, your routine agendas. Sanctify your saints, solidify your soldiers, settle your differences, separate your chaff, situate your troops, and send your messengers as never before!

Make your plans unbelievably large; stretch your faith to incredible lengths; pray your prayers with undying unction; and march your army with impeccable precision. The lines of battle are now drawn, the enemy strong, the battle relentless, the hour late, the soldiers few, but the opportunity great.

O dear Church, dispense with 'business as usual.' It's time to proclaim, not procrastinate, pursue, not postpone; lunge, not linger; march, not meet; advance, not retreat. It's time to win, not waver; to claim, not cower; to conquer, not capitulate; to capture not carouse; to be concerned, not complacent. I'm coming soon, I hope you're ready!

Jesus

SPECIAL SEASONS

Birthdays, anniversaries, Christmas, Easter, the 4th of July, Thanksgiving....what do they all have in common? They're special seasons. Youth, the middle years, and even old age are all special seasons. The arrival of a first child is a special season (the arrival of any child is a special season). Life is filled with special seasons, special times, special occasions, special dinners, special get-to-gethers. Cherish them, they're not that many in number. Savor them when they come, for they leave so quickly. Capture them on film, for once they're over, they're over. Anticipate the next one. No one ever regretted, at the end of their life, that they spent too much time with their families, their friends, and their memories. Special occasions are like a majestic sunset, awesome, breathtaking, but oh, so soon over!

A New Year's Prayer

Lord, this is the last day of an old year. I stand before You like a piling under a wharf that has gathered unsightly barnacles and debris. Lord, today, clean out my life and make me fit to walk into a new year, clean and unencumbered. Scrape from my heart the burdensome barnacles of all my botches and bungling. Strip from my life all the unbecoming garments of pride, arrogance and ego. As a gardener, O Lord, pull from my life today all that is unbecoming; all the weeks and months of worry; the roots of resistance; the burgeoning briers of bullheadedness and the vines of vexation.

Before the New Year arrives, disinfect the dirtiness of my deeds, destroy the detestable, destructive debris of my life, clear from my agenda all that is mundane, mediocre and moldy. Peel from my spirit, O Lord, all the layers of lewdness, lusting and lying. Scrub away, O God, all that is sullied, stained, septic and soiled. Repaint today, O Lord, my faded walls; restore just now my voice; unstop my tongue to speak Your praise; wash away the haze that I may see You lifted up. Remove from my life this day, Lord, all that is small, rebellious, obstinate and unsurrendered to You.

Sweep out of my life all that is unimportant, unnecessary, unnatural and all that is ugly. Clear my mind of all thinking that is negative and unproductive. Breathe into me the fresh breath of Your Spirit and rib me with the steel of Your courage to face the New Year with a dogged determination to stand at the center of Your will all the way through. Give me eyes to see beyond the physical, ears to hear beyond the audible, hands to touch hurting people, feet to speed to those in need, eyes to see those opportunities, Lord, that You see. Lord, I pull the shade on an old year and raise the shade to a new one. Grant me wisdom to walk with You and not look back.

Amen

DECEMBER PRAYER

Dear God, deliver me from the phony Christmas, the one that reaches its materialistic tentacles out to capture me and rob me of the real thing. Deliver me from the mania and madness of harried schedules, from frantic shopping...the acquiring of goods for people who don't need them, don't want them, won't wear them and can't use them...save me from the folly of mood changes brought on by holly, mistletoe, wreathes, boughs and eggnog. For once, O God, clear my ears of the ringing of the cash register and the clanging of bells and in their place let me hear the angel's song. For once let me fill my soul with the reading of the Christ-child, the wisemen, the angels, and the star instead of feeding my body on fruit cake and caloried candies and cakes. O Lord, don't let me fall prey again to all the trappings of the season to the point that I miss the real event. Lord, deliver me from over-fondness of food, a yen to party, the urge to spend with the plastic cards, and the temptation to overdo it in every department.

And Lord, in the giving and exchanging of myriads of gifts, let me not forget to give a worthy gift to Him whose birthday it really is.

Amen

GRADUATION: A PARENT'S PERSPECTIVE

What's that I see...a cap and gown...a diploma in your hand? The tassel moved...as the deep voice announces 'degree granted.' Is that you my son, you look like a man...where is the little boy whose chubby hand I held when you fell a thousand times learning to walk? Are you the same boy whose hair I cut at age one? When your mother cried, so did I!

O time, what have you done to me? O years, it went all too quickly; why is it over already? Are you the same boy who shyly went out for the team and were surprised when the coach said, 'you made it?' Oh, the wagons, the bikes, the balls, the bats, the mitts, the games; the endless chauffeuring, the first driving test; the jalopy you bought, the camps, the college trips back and forth, the holidays.

O time, is that a man I see on the stage? It can't be my son, but it is...O years, when he was only four you dragged by so slowly, what's your hurry now? I walk into his room...I see the bare walls where posters used to be...I see an empty closet. It looks so strange — your bed is made, your room is clean and tidy.

O years, bring back the mess, the noise, the commotion; this silence is so deafening. No more fast meals, no more dirty clothes. No more late night ping-pong parties, the curtain has fallen, the course is over; I've raised a son, tall, proud, godly but now gone.

Oh time, I could shake you...but then again, I love you...you've matured a man.

O God, I release my son to you, he's gone and my shaping and molding days are over.

Amen

THE TIMES

If our forefathers missed the stagecoach to Dodge City, they went home and waited two weeks for the next one. If we miss one turn in a revolving door, we have a nervous breakdown!

No one really understands the complexity of the times in which we live. In one sense they are the worst of times, but in another sense they are the best of times. One thing is for sure...no previous generation was more stressed, more prone to nerve problems, more prone to depression or more confused than ours. One cynical writer has called this generation the "cut-flower" generation. Nothing lasts for very long. Short-term commitments, short-term employment, short-term marriages, short-term addresses, and short-term relationships seem to be indicative of the times.

But, through it all, we have the assurance of knowing that a sovereign God is controlling the watch, the calendar, and all our activities. That is why the Psalmist could say, "My times are in your hands" (Psalm 31:15). He hasn't left the controls; He didn't create us to abandon us. He has promised never to leave us or forsake us. No wonder we are told in scripture to "number our days that we may get a heart of wisdom."

The times may be shaky, but the absolutes given in God's Word aren't. How essential it is today for everyone to find that "rock" that won't move no matter how much the wind blows and the waves batter. That rock is Christ!

THE PARADOX OF OUR AGE

We have taller buildings but shorter tempers; wider freeways but narrower viewpoints; we spend more but have less; we buy more but enjoy it less; we have bigger houses and smaller families; more conveniences, yet less time; we have more degrees but less sense; more knowledge but less judgment; more experts, yet more problems; we have more gadgets but less satisfaction; more medicine, yet less wellness; we take more vitamins but see fewer results. We drink too much; smoke too much; spend too recklessly; laugh too little; drive too fast; get too angry quickly; stay up too late; get up too tired; read too seldom; watch TV too much and pray too seldom.

We have multiplied our possessions, but reduced our values; we fly in faster planes to arrive there quicker, to do less and return sooner; we sign more contracts only to realize fewer profits; we talk too much; love too seldom and lie too often. We've learned how to make a living, but not a life; we've added years to life, not life to years. We've been all the way to the moon and back, but have trouble crossing the street to meet the new neighbor. We've conquered outer space, but not inner space; we've done larger things, but not better things; we've cleaned up the air, but polluted the soul; we've split the atom, but not our prejudice; we write more, but learn less; plan more, but accomplish less; we make faster planes, but longer lines; we learned to rush, but not to wait; we have more weapons, but less peace; higher incomes, but lower morals; more parties, but less fun; more food, but less appeasement; more acquaintances, but fewer friends; more effort, but less success. We build more computers to hold more information, to produce more copies than ever, but have less communication; drive smaller cars that have bigger problems; build larger factories that produce less. We've become long on quantity, but short on quality.

These are the times of fast foods and slow digestion; tall men, but short character; steep in profits, but shallow relationships. These are times of world peace, but domestic warfare; more leisure and less fun; higher postage, but slower mail; more kinds of food, but less nutrition. These are days of two incomes, but more divorces; these are times of fancier houses, but broken homes. These are days of quick trips, disposable diapers, cartridge living, throw-away morality, one-night stands, overweight bodies and pills that do everything from cheer, to prevent, quiet or kill. It is a time when there is much in the show window and nothing in the stock room. Indeed, these are the times!

.